progressive parenting

The Definitive Resource Book

progressive parenting

The Definitive Resource Book

John Parankimalil

Publisher
UNICORN BOOKS

F-2/16, Ansari Road, Daryaganj, New Delhi-110002
☎ 011-23275434, 23262683, 23250704 • *Fax:* 011-23257790
E-mail: info@unicornbooks.in • *Website:* www.unicornbooks.in

Branch : Mumbai
23-25, Zaoba Wadi Thakurdwar, Mumbai-401002
☎ 022-22010941, 022-22053387
E-mail: rapidex@bom5.vsnl.net.in

Showroom :
★ **PM Publications,** New Delhi
- 10-B, Netaji Subhash Marg, Daryaganj
  New Delhi-110002
- 6686, Khari Baoli, Delhi-110006

Distributors :
★ **Pustak Mahal,** New Delhi
Delhi: ☎ 011-23276539
Bengaluru: ☎ 080-22234025
Patna: ☎ 0612-3294193

★ **V & S Publishers,** Hyderabad
☎ 040-24737290

ISBN 978-81-7806-149-8
Progressive Parenting
Edition: 2012

Printed at: Param offsetters, Okhla, New Delhi-110020

The book is dedicated to my beloved parents
Devassy** and **Thresia,
who taught me through their life
and example.

Acknowledgements

This book is a result of my interaction with several parents and students during my 14 long years of experience in St. Anthony's Higher Secondary School, Shillong. Much of the contents of this book are anecdotes recounted from stories that have appeared elsewhere, in books, magazines, newspapers, periodicals and from my very own inbox. Some of the stories have been handed down to us over generations; others have been inspired by and adapted from other speakers and various published material.

While every effort has been made to attribute credit to the original author, sources were not always recorded and hence it was impossible to provide a detailed acknowledgement. Nonetheless, I would like to express my gratitude to all who have contributed to this work.

I offer my sincere gratitude and appreciation to Mr. Sanjay Sharma, editor and publisher, for his guidance and encouragement. It is largely due to his efforts, boundless enthusiasm and dedication that this book was brought out in record time. I also thank Mr. Durlabh Bhattacharjee for his fine illustrations.

I have been especially inspired by the writings of Derek and Michelle Brookes, Pervin Dadachanji, Juliet Thomas, Pat Holt, Connie Grigsby and Kent Julian, Patt and Steve Saso and Mary Kay Mueller. My sincere thanks to them.

John Parankimalil

Foreword

Parenting today can seem harder and scarier than ever with the pressing work demands and busy family schedules, the attractions and distractions of electronic media, and the real threats to older children and adolescents of school violence, substance and alcohol abuse, and other risky behaviours.

But the greatest joy in this world are also children. Without children this world will be ruined. Children hold within their beings the amazing propensity to delight and enthrall and can also be a never-ending source of joy and wonderment. Sadly, children are among the worst sufferers in modern times particularly due to abuse and neglect. They suffer in peacetime and in war, in the change of season and in natural catastrophe, at home and in the community; but are soon sidelined and forgotten, the silent sufferers in the march of time.

The happiness, sanctity and joy of tomorrow's world depends largely upon the children of today — the citizens of tomorrow. It rests upon the shoulders of the Youth to make the world heaven or hell. What a huge responsibility today's parents have in bringing up their children in the proper way.

There are many books on how to raise children but today's generation gap is very wide. Therefore it is absolutely essential these books are available to meet the requirements of the new generation. Parents must equip themselves as best they can to raise their children in discipline, to equip them adequately to face a cruel and difficult world and be protected from wrong influences.

This book covers certain vital aspects of parenting. Parents, specially in those households where both are employed outside the home, are sure to find the chapters on spending time with their young ones, being role models, helping their children deal with peer pressure and listening to them most relevant and useful.

It is indeed most gratifying that my good friend, Fr. P.D. Johny has made such a marvellous effort at a time when it is needed the most. The painstaking manner in which he has pieced together the contents and structured its chapters are indeed praiseworthy. Fr. Johny started his career in St. Anthony's Higher Secondary School where he came across thousands of parents, children, teenagers and had the joy of counselling and guiding them. This book, then, is not just a testimony of academic knowledge but the evidence of the one-and-a-half decades of experience of fruitful ministry.

Progressive Parenting is bound to prove an invaluable resource and a repository of inspiration for progressive parents wanting to raise their children as healthy, wholesome, upright human beings. I hope parents will make judicious use of the tips and counsel that has been put together in an immensely readable form in Fr. Johny's latest offering.

Ranjan Chatterjee, *IAS*
Chief Secretary
Government of Meghalaya

Table of Contents

PART III : Mailwise

Introduction

Kids! Precious kids, wonderful kids, naughty kids, happy kids! If you have kids, they have changed your life. One reason for this is that they need you so much. In the beginning they are helpless and depend totally on you. Little by little they start to grow up, but they still need you a lot and look to you for help and answers — at least until they start getting older and becoming more independent.

"Being a parent isn't easy!" said a scripture scholar, "It takes the strength of Samson; the wisdom of Solomon; the patience of Job; the insight of Daniel; the courage, determination, and leadership of King David; the faith of Abraham — and most of all, the love of God!" Parenting has never been easy; today's complex world with its fast-paced changes compounds it further.

Today's world is a morass of confusing messages and troubling images that stir up a maelstrom of emotions in the very young. As your little ones grow, you may often be ridden with uncertainty and self-doubt. How on earth can you protect them from the harsh and insensitive world around them; how are you going to instil in them the values of love, obedience, respect and positivism to hold them in good stead when much of what they are surrounded by is diametrically opposite!

Movies, TV, video and computer games, advertising, music, troubled peers and lately the Internet individually and together contribute to a growing moral pandemonium that can have a catastrophic effect on children. Many of the influences your children are exposed to not only fail to teach wholesome values, but actively encourage wrong attitudes and behaviour. It is not surprising then, that the news is increasingly dominated by headlines of children having committed terrible crimes, often without any apparent pangs of conscience or remorse. Their parents are

increasingly being blamed — and in some cases even held legally responsible — for their children's delinquency. Ironically, though, while parents are being held accountable for their children's conduct, they are consistently being stripped of their moral right to exercise their discretion as parents to remedy recalcitrance and discipline their children.

Contemporary times thrust an onerous responsibility on 21st-century parents of nuclear families. The greatest pride for any parent, I suppose, is a child with proper upbringing, and on the flip side, the greatest sorrow a wayward child. It is imperative, therefore, that parents equip themselves with whatever skills necessary to raise their children in a manner that prepares them to take on all that the world throws at them without breaking stride. Above all, ensuring that they emerge from such battles scarred, perhaps, but stronger and more resolute.

The cornerstone to successful child rearing remains the same — love, that wonder salve that can heal the most mortal wounds! The miracle of God's love, the love you have for your children, their love for you; and the love that they will in turn learn to have for others. It is the lessons rooted in the subconscious of their formative years that will eventually steer your children through life, helping them make the right choices, taking the right decisions and treading the righteous path. Love will steady them through the tumult of growing up and be an antidote to the negative influences they encounter. Love will give them purpose and passion; steadfastness and direction; grit and determination.

I write this book in the firm belief that its contents will serve as a resource book for progressive parents who want to guide and mould their children into the image and likeness of God Himself.

John Parankimalil

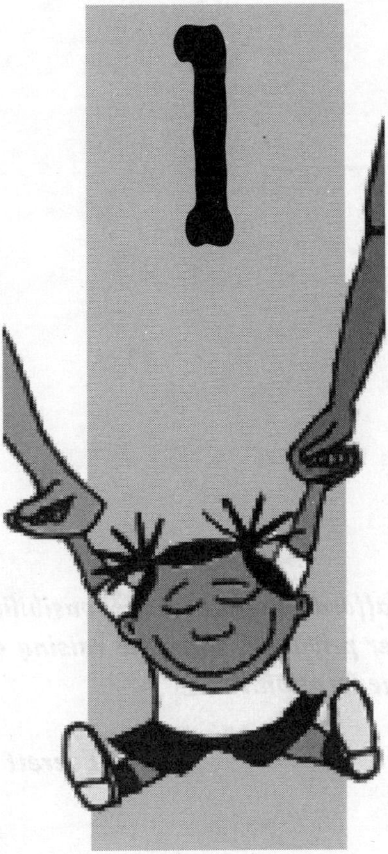

UNDERSTANDING PARENTAL PRIVILEGES AND RESPONSIBILITIES

"Life affords no greater responsibility, no greater privilege, than the raising of the next generation."

C. Everett Koop

CHAPTER ONE

There is no greater evidence of a miracle than a baby; a tiny and complete little bundle of human life. Destined for manhood or womanhood, made in the image of God and a judicious mix of both its parents, every little life is marked by character, temperament and identity that gives it an individuality and uniqueness of its own.

In case of a first-born, a husband and wife go from being just man and wife to father and mother. The couple metamorphoses into a family almost overnight adding a new member to the household and a new bough to the family tree. The home is never the same!

Mark Twain described a baby as ***"an inestimable blessing and bother."*** The seemingly interminable ritual of changing diapers, feeding rituals and midnight bawling eventually make way for teething trouble, the first unsteady steps and baby prattle followed by the nerve-wracking job of keeping things out of reach of curious little fingers! Then, almost before their parents can realise it, children are off to school, adolescence close on its heels. It is a bittersweet feeling of joy tinged with sadness as what was once a wailing bundle of helplessness matures into an adolescent and then a young adult, standing at the crossroads of life, awaiting acceptance and approval in society.

What kind of adult will (s)he be? Will (s)he be kind or cruel? Will (s)he build or destroy? Will (s)he wound or heal? And above all, when (s)he is gone, how will (s)he be remembered — with fondness, respect or abhorrence?

Parents hold the answer to some of these questions; for they are the sculptors who knead and mould the personalities of their children during their formative years giving them shape and definition to carve a niche for themselves in the community.

The road to child-rearing is littered with obstacles and pitfalls that seem to conspire against parents' efforts to rear a healthy, wholesome, righteous individual who will contribute his or her mite to society. Done right, parenting also wields the potential of bringing tremendous joy; when offspring are reared in a balanced atmosphere of temperance and propriety it yields an immense sense of gratification.

What is parenting?

Parenting — the process of raising and educating a child from birth till adulthood — is gaining popularity as a topic of discussion today, since urban lifestyles force a clear distinction between caring for a child in the home vis-à-vis the formal education (s)he receives at school. Logically, since a teacher-student relationship differs markedly from a parent-child relationship, it follows that a

child's education at home must be different from its education at school. This is true. What parents, teach their children at home is guided by the same ideology and principles as the instruction they receive at school. The content of parental instruction determines the intrinsic facets of their personality, traits and attributes, or ***'who'*** they become as against scholastic instruction or ***'what'*** they become professionally — in terms of skills, aptitudes, accolades, credentials and achievements. At school, teachers impart knowledge that give a child general literacy and scientific knowledge while at home parents give a child general wisdom of life as they themselves understand it. Simply put, it is the difference between intelligence quotient (IQ) and emotional quotient or EQ!

'Parenting' is a verb derivative of the noun *'parent.'* Thus, the phrase *'parent a child'* actually means to be a parent to a child or to fulfil parental obligations. A large majority are in agreement that parents' primary duties towards their children have to do with fulfilling their basic needs: primarily security and development. This would imply not just physical security but a notional sense of being inviolable! It may also be construed as development in the holistic sense; that is growth in moral, spiritual, intellectual, emotional, psychological and physiological terms.

Since the male and female progenitors of an offspring are its biological parents, a mother and father are conventionally considered the primary providers of *'parenting.'* But there are exceptions to this rule and when parents are either incapable, unwilling or simply not present, close relatives, such as older siblings, aunts and uncles or grandparents quickly step in as surrogates to care for a child. Where children are abandoned or orphaned, they may be fostered by adoptive parents or collectively cared for in institutions such as children's homes or orphanages.

Parenting although ranked among the most thrilling, rewarding experiences of life does pose some of the greatest challenges. Much of it stems from the inherent human trend of 'expectation!' More often than not, parents tend to be idealistic and want only the very best for their child. They want to do more for their child and give more than they themselves have had. Each desires to be someone their child needs, loves, admires, respects, and perhaps even wants to be like. Deep down, they harbour a secret wish that they have given birth to and are raising a prodigy; they are loath to accept any inadequacy or failing in their child and seem blind to fault. They are fiercely protective and tend to disregard transgressions as passing, inconsequential aberrations. In doing so, however, they unwittingly sow the first seeds of leniency with far-reaching and often damaging consequences on a child's subconscious.

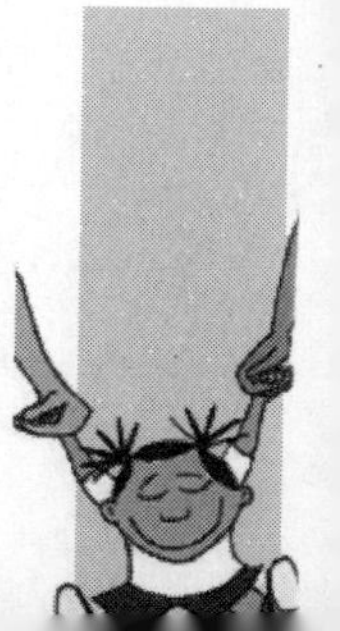

Part of the joy of parenting comes from exploring and rediscovering life with their child. It is almost like revisiting one's own childhood and viewing from a fresh perspective, the energy, enthusiasm, need, and dependency that builds an almost inseparable bond and fuels the passion to be model parents.

All too often though, parents' idealism fades in the hurly-burly of life where personal and financial problems, emotional demands and professional commitments among other things, take precedence over the esoteric and abstract. Pipe dreams are relegated to the backseat by the ruthless machinations of an unforgiving world. It is in these moments of disillusionment, despondence and near despair that parents need to reach for the keys that open the doors of hope and love; love in such abundance that it touches their lives and the lives of their children leaving them transformed for all time.

Parental duties

Let us now return to the main issue of parental duties and responsibilities. Once the initial stage of giving birth and nurturing a newborn from infancy to childhood has passed, parents enter a stage critical to the development of a child. We have already determined that the primary responsibility of parents is to ensure physical security and development for their children by providing them adequate shelter, clothing and

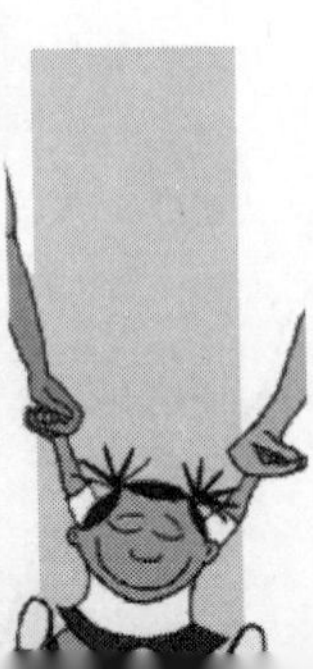

nourishment. To safeguard them against threats — real or perceived — and to ensure that they are not only secure in the physical sense but even ***feel*** warm, safe and comfortable in parental sanctuary. The importance of this sense of well-being during childhood can hardly be over-emphasised in adulthood.

Most profilers usually trace the roots of adult psychology or behavioural patterns to the Petri dish of their childhood, where, the degree and frequency of occurrence of pleasant or traumatic incidents are directly proportionate to their own nature and temperament.

Perpetrators of crimes that are exceptionally brutal or gory in nature are usually individuals who have had troubled or abusive childhoods. Events such as sexual abuse, neglect or emotional battery that has left terrible scars on their psyche. Other effects of childhood grooming or upbringing can be gauged, for example, from an individual's personal hygiene, amiability, sociability and overall disposition.

Parents must also ensure that the intellectual security and development of the child is not impinged upon in any way that is likely to have an adverse effect in the long run.

Intellectual security refers to an atmosphere that is congenial for the development of a child's build-up and mental ability. It means providing a

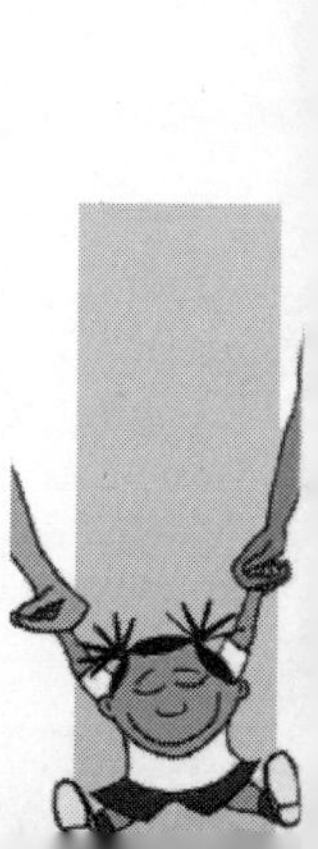

child with the opportunity to learn in a manner that not only moulds its powers of comprehension and reasoning but also provides it with the building blocks to form an opinion of its own and sharpen its own finer sensibilities.

Besides being taught reading, writing and calculating, a child needs to be exposed to an environment that becomes a training and testing ground for social skills and etiquette, ethics and value systems in a manner that will contribute to its adult persona.

If the child's dignity is safeguarded so that nobody may intimidate it physically or verbally, then an environment conducive to learning has been effectively provided for. It is important that a child experience an atmosphere of peace and justice in the family hierarchy, where all members have individual positions conferring upon them the respect and dignity that is commensurate with their importance and standing.

Another important responsibility of the parent is to provide emotional security to the child in a manner that shields it from trauma in any shape or form by building trust and reassurance. It ought to be borne in mind, however, that while it is important to provide a warm, secure cocoon as a sanctuary of safety for a child, it is equally if not more important that the child not be cloistered from the harsh realities of the world outside.

Thus, while providing a safe, loving environment conveys to a child a readymade support system where (s)he is loved, needed, wanted and welcomed unconditionally, (s)he must be made strong and independent enough to be able to hold his/her own without any external help. This is best described as emotional development since it teaches a child to trust, but with caution, to love but with prudence, to help without expecting reward and to care for those who have no way of reciprocating. In short, it lays the foundation for a child to exercise discretion and objectivity in all manner of dealings.

"What God is to the world, parents are to their children."

Philo

100 WAYS TO SAY 'WELL DONE'

CAROL WEBSTER

That's super
Spot on
I like it
Super stuff
Really great
What a good try
Brilliant
Clever (boy/girl)
I'm impressed
What a brainwave
You do work well
Very imaginative
Nice try
That's good work
Superb
Well remembered
Good logic
Excellent work
Good thinking
You're a star
You are doing well
Great try
Quick thinking
Well done
Well figured out
I like that
Congratulations
You are doing great
You've done really well
Keep on trying
You show real promise
You have great ideas
You've mastered it

Well thought out
You've fitted a lot in
How imaginative you are
Good problem solving
What a perfect example
Well worked through
I'm very proud of you
I'm proud of your work
You're really tuned in today
A very good try
You learn quickly
You really stuck with it
You don't give up
Beautiful job
That's good thinking
You've got the hang of it
You've done better than ever
That's a fine attempt
You're a problem solver
I couldn't have done better myself
You soon mastered that
You've got that down to a fine art
Pleasure to see you work like that
One more try and you'll be there
You're work is improving
You are a pleasure to teach

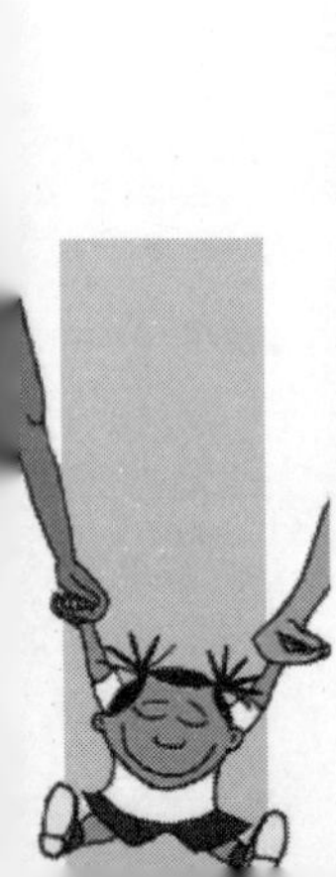

USING PRAISE & APPRECIATION EFFECTIVELY

"If you want your children to improve, let them overhear the nice things you say about them to others."

Haim Ginott

CHAPTER TWO

The first vital 'behaviour-shaper' of a child is praise and appreciation. Any behaviour that is rewarded will invariably be repeated, while behaviour that is frowned upon or goes unrewarded is bound to decline. According to **Sir William James,** *"The deepest principle of human nature is the craving to be appreciated."* In a similar vein, **Mark Twain** says, *"I can live for two months on a good compliment."* Simple words and actions of affirmation, appreciation and support can be a tremendously powerful investment in children's lives. Children thrive on praise and encouragement. Sometimes children will throw tantrums or behave in a churlish, petulant manner simply to grab attention.

Appreciation is the finest and most effective parental tool. What children seek the most from their parents is recognition — credit for their efforts. If you do that, your children will live for you and even break their backs trying to gain your approval.

Publius Syrus says, *"Admonish your children privately, but praise them openly."* This is further qualified in what **Sam Walton** has to say on the subject: *"Nothing else can quite substitute for a few well-chosen, well-timed, sincere words of praise. They're absolutely free — and worth a fortune."*

*When **Sir Walter Scott** was a boy, he was considered a dull student, and often found himself in Coventry facing the ignominy of sitting in a corner donning the dunce's high-pointed paper cap of shame. As a lad of 12 or 14, Scott happened to be in the house where Robert Burns, the Scottish poet, and some others were being entertained. Burns stood admiring a picture that piqued his interest. Reading the couple of lines of verse beneath the canvas, he inquired who the author was but no one seemed to know. Timidly a boy sidled up to him, tugged at his coat and not only named the author but even recited the rest of the poem. Burns was both surprised and delighted. Laying his hand on the boy's head, he exclaimed, "Ah, Bairnie, you will be a great man in Scotland some day!" From that day onward, Walter Scott was a changed person. A simple word of encouragement had set him on the road to greatness!*

(Author Unknown)

Whenever your child does something well, make it a point to express your appreciation. If your child scores 100 in Mathematics, say, "You've done well. Keep it up!" If your child has given her new dress to a poor girl, keeps her stuff neatly or assists in a routine household chore, make it a point to tell her how much you appreciate her gesture.

Many years ago, a boy of 10 was working in a factory in Naples. He longed to be a singer, but his first

teacher discouraged him. "You can't sing," he said, "You haven't any voice at all. It sounds like the wind in the shutters." The boy's mother, a poor peasant woman, had more faith in her son. She put her arms around the boy and bade him not to lose heart. She knew he could sing, she told him, and could already see an improvement. Then she went barefoot in order to save money to pay for his music lessons. That peasant mother's praise and encouragement changed the boy's life. His name was ***Enrico Caruso,*** *and he became the most famous opera singer of his time.*
(Dale Carnegie)

Praise the behaviour, not the person. General phrases like *"good girl"* or *"clever boy"* risk being misinterpreted. A child may feel that if (s)he doesn't do well, (s)he is bad. Saying, *"You did a good job cleaning your room,"* or *"I like the way you've used so much colour in this picture,"* makes the praise sound sincere, since it demonstrates encouragement for the special nature of the act.

Be realistic. If you praise every move your child makes, (s)he will either get addicted or start doubting your sincerity. Praise should sound spontaneous to prevent it from being viewed as an affectation. Should your daughter disinterestedly kick around a football and you remark *"Great kick!"* she is bound to doubt your genuineness.

Change praise. Children have a short attention span and tire easily. To keep a child absorbed, change the tone and tenor of how you deliver praise. You can convey this not only with words but also through appreciative non-verbal gestures. A simple thumbs-up or a short note applauding a change you have noticed in the child's behaviour goes a long way. Kids are thrilled by positive messages addressed to them.

Referential talk. The way adults discuss children has an even more powerful effect on young behaviour than direct praise or attention. This is called referential speaking — conversation that takes place between parents, or between a parent and teacher or other important adult figures, within the child's hearing. Referential speaking can be positive or negative. Saying something like, *"Banri Kupar is not as clever as his sister; that's why he doesn't do too well"* (with Banri Kupar within earshot) is referential speaking that makes a child feel inadequate or incapable. The same statement could be paraphrased to: *"I notice that Banri Kupar is really working as hard as his sister to do well,"* not only makes him feel good about himself but will also urge him to do better. When you see something positive about your child, share it with someone. When you notice the negative, downplay or ignore it. At any rate, avoid discussing the matter if children are within hearing range.

While praise, used in the appropriate manner and at opportune time, can have a positive influence in shaping behaviour, it is not the only way to reinforce good conduct. In some ways, it is

superficial. Praise is an external motivator. The ultimate goal of discipline is self-discipline and inner motivation. One instance illustrating this would be: praising good grades to give young minds the idea that great school results are the ticket to success. Let's try looking at it this way. Eventually, a child attempts to secure good marks mainly to secure approval, thereby making the child happy.

> ***"Praise your children openly, reprehend them secretly."***
>
> ***W. Cecil***

3

SPENDING QUALITY TIME WITH YOUR CHILDREN

"In bringing up children, spend on them half as much money and twice as much time."

Anonymous

CHAPTER THREE

You may have heard of the adage **"Time is Money,"** but how much value **your** time holds for your children or how precious it is to them is something you might never be able to fathom! What most children crave the most is quality time with their parents. Your children will never forget the special time they spend with you. You don't always have to spend a great deal of time with children to make them know you love and appreciate them. It is not the duration but the quality of the time you spend with them that makes a difference to your children. Time is perhaps the greatest investment you can make in your children. It also happens to be the greatest gift you can give them, because nothing else makes a more lasting difference in their lives. As **Jesse Jackson** succinctly put it, *"Your children need your presence more than your presents."* Play with your children, read with them, hold them, encourage them, and enjoy them; go for walks or just sit around together and talk; ask questions and listen to their answers — don't simply hear; really listen — and see the difference it makes!

Determine how much time you need to spend with each of your children each week, and factor it into your schedule. Accord it top priority, an inviolate appointment that must be kept at all costs. If a ***genuine*** emergency comes up, you could consider rescheduling your time with your children; postpone but don't cancel! According to

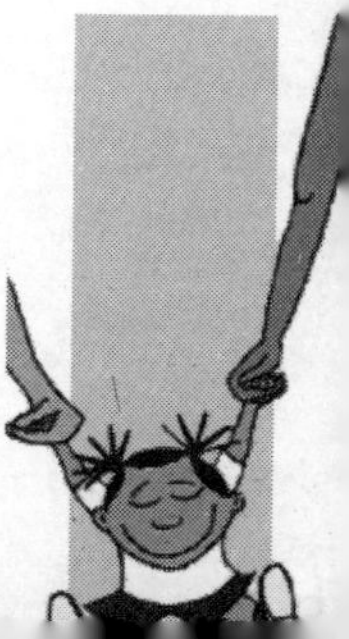

TIME
TIME
TIME
TIME

Orlando A. Battista, *"The best inheritance a parent can give to his children is a few minutes of his time each day."*

> *A successful young attorney said, "The greatest gift I ever received came in a very small box as light as a feather. My dad gave it to me one Christmas. Inside the box was a note that read as follows: 'Son, this year I will give you 365 hours. An hour every day after dinner is yours. We'll talk about what you want to talk about, we'll go where you want to go, play what you want to play. It will be your hour!' My dad not only kept that promise, but renewed it every year. That was the greatest gift anyone ever gave me. I am the result of his time."*
> **(Cited in Moody Monthly)**

When older children are confronted by the pangs of growing up or other adolescent problems, they need even more of your time, and you need to be even more attentive to their needs — which are very often not even verbalised. This touching story bears repeating to drive the point home.

> *With a timid voice and adoring eyes, the little boy greeted his father as he returned from work, "Daddy, how much do you make an hour?"*
> *Surprised, at the tenor and attitude of the questioner, the father shot back, "Look, son, not even your mother knows that; don't bother me now, it's been a long day and I'm tired."*

"But Daddy, just tell me please! How much do you make an hour," the boy persisted.

Finally giving up, the father replied: "Twenty dollars an hour."

"Okay, Daddy?" the boy reasoned, "Could you loan me $10?"

Restless by now and positively agitated, the father yelled: "So that's why you asked how much I earn? Go to sleep and don't bother me anymore!"

The boy fell silent and withdrew to his room where he turned out the light and crept under the coverlets. Before long the father began feeling the pangs of remorse and reflected on what he had said to his son. Maybe, he really needed to buy something. Unable to suppress his guilt any longer, the father padded into his son's room.

"Are you asleep, son?" asked the father. "No, Daddy," grunted the boy drowsily, "Why?"

"Here's the money you asked for earlier," the father said dipping into the pocket of his pyjamas and proferring a $10 bill. "Thanks, Daddy!" the son said excitedly. Slipping his hand under the pillow he quickly brought it back out. "Now I have $20!" the boy said to his father, who seemed a little confused at his son's behaviour. "Daddy," he looked up imploringly at his father, "Could I buy just one hour of your time only for myself?"

You may have heard this story. Many of you may find it contrived. You may be very busy individuals but there's a moral here. Make it a point to spend quality time with your children. Talk to them. Listen to them. Occasionally, take them to places of interest. It will make them feel they are as important as all your other interests. You may be interested in your business, but your child would prefer to play. You must be prepared to sacrifice your time for the sake of your little ones.

*American novelist **O Henry** has a story in which he tells of a little girl whose mother had passed away when she was little. Her father would come home from work and sit down to read the newspapers. The little girl would come in and ask him to play with her for a little while, because she felt lonely but each time she asked, he replied: "I'm tired now. Leave me in peace and go play outside." The little girl began to play in the streets. Before she knew it, she fell into bad times and took to the streets.*

The years passed. She died and went to heaven. Upon the arrival of the girl's soul there, she was received by St Peter who brought her before the Lord and said: "Master, here's a girl who has led life without virtue and full of sin, surely she is going straight to hell?"

"No," replied the Lord, to the astonishment of St Peter, "Let her in," he said, "but look for a man who refused to play with his little daughter when she needed him and instead sent her out into the streets to fend for herself; that's the man that goes straight to hell!"

A survey was made among 300 seventh and eighth grade boys for a two-week period to discover how much time fathers and sons spent together. Each boy kept an accurate record of the time spent with his father. The boys that 'met Dad only at the Dinner table' comprised the largest group. A number of boys never saw their fathers for days at a time, some not even for weeks. The average time father and son had alone together for an entire week was seven minutes!

> ***Lovasik*** *tells about a doctor who was busy in his study when his small son came in and stood silently by his side. The doctor, busy with his work, put his hand into his pocket, took out a coin and offered it to the lad. "I don't want any money, Daddy," the boy said.*
>
> *Still finding him standing by his side, the doctor opened a drawer of his desk withdrew a bar of chocolate and offered this to his son. Again the lad refused to take it but stayed by his father's side.*
>
> *Growing a little impatient, the doctor turned to him, a look of exasperation on his face... "Well, what do you want, then?"*
>
> *"Nothing," replied the boy, a little confused, "I only want to be with you!"*

LOVING YOUR CHILDREN

"Making the decision to have a child is momentous. It is to decide forever to have your heart go walking around outside your body."

Elizabeth Stone

CHAPTER FOUR

Let your children know that you love them unconditionally. Unconditional love is what makes children happy and gives them the capacity to look beyond personality deficiencies and human error. There are parents whose love is almost superficially pre-conditional; solely based upon their children's performance. Your love for your children should be non-negotiable and brook no bargain. Your love should convey to your children the feeling that you are there for them regardless of anything, and that you are always available to give them the support they may need for their development, no matter what. Love values the other for what (s)he is, not because (s)he is something you want or expect him/her to be. All human beings, for that matter, from newborn to adult, need to receive love without conditions.

When **Jackie DeShannon** sang, *"What the world needs now is love, sweet love,"* most of her generation sang along with her. According to her song, the world doesn't need any more mountains to climb or rivers to cross. What we need is love, *"not just for some, but for everyone."* **Kenny Rogers** sang a love song titled, ***'You Decorated My Life.'*** His lyrics celebrated the way our lives are enhanced when we are loved. Parents today need to decorate their children's lives with a love that is pure and sincere. The cure for all the ills and wrongs, the cares, the sorrows and crimes of humanity, all lie in that one word 'Love.'

Mother Teresa mentioned to a group of visitors that once a little boy had come to her convent around midnight. As she opened the door, he broke down saying: "I went to my mother and she didn't want me; I went to my father and he didn't want me...you...do you want me?" Unless there is real love between parents, unconditional love will not flow to their children.

> *Newspaper columnist and minister* ***George Crane*** *tells of a wife who came into his office full of hatred toward her husband. "I not only want to get rid of him," she cried, "I want to get even! Before I divorce him, I want to hurt him as much as he has hurt me!"*
>
> *Dr. Crane suggested an ingenious plan "Go home and act as if you really love your husband. Tell him how much he means to you. Praise him for every decent trait. Go out of your way to be as kind, considerate, and generous as possible. Spare no efforts to please him, to enjoy him. Make him believe you love him. After you've convinced him of your undying love and that you cannot live without him, and then drop the bomb. Tell him that you're getting a divorce. That will really hurt him." With revenge in her eyes, she smiled and exclaimed, "Beautiful, beautiful. Will he ever be surprised?" And she did it with enthusiasm, acting as if she did. For two months she showed love, kindness, listening, giving,*

reinforcing, sharing. When she didn't return, Crane called her. "Are you ready now to go through with the divorce?"

"Divorce?" she exclaimed. "Never! I discovered I really do love him." Her actions had changed her feelings. Motion resulted in emotion. The ability to love is established not so much by fervent promise as by oft repeated deeds.

Children who get their needs for love and attention fulfilled at home have far fewer problems than those who need to seek elsewhere. Assure your children that you will continue to love them no matter what they do, and that you will be there for them. Part of that love is not allowing them to do things that you know to be harmful, but at the same time reassuring them that you will never stop loving them. When your children put you to the test and find that your love holds even when they displease you, this helps them feel secure. They will then be more likely to stand up against negative peer pressure and make the right decision the next time.

I would like to recount here a touching story I read from ***Second Helping of Chicken Soup for the Soul*** *about* The Flower. *The story is narrated by* ***Pastor John R. Ramsey.*** *After he was transferred to a new church, a friend of his used to give him a flower every Sunday before the service to wear on his coat lapel. It had become so routine and ordinary for him to receive the flower that he never gave it any* *thought. One day, a little boy named Jimmy stopped him after the service and asked him, 'Sir, what are you going to do with your flower?' At first the pastor did not know what to say. Before he could answer, the child interrupted, 'Sir, if you are going to throw it away please give it to me.' The pastor told him that he would be indeed glad to give away the flower. The pastor then asked the boy to tell him what was he going to do with the flower? Jimmy said, 'Sir, I want to give this flower to my granny. Today is her birthday and I love her very much.' The pastor said, "Jimmy, please tell me more about your granny." So Jimmy continued, "My father and mother got divorced last year. I was living with my mother, but when she got married again, she wanted me to live with my father. I lived with him for a while, but he said that I could not stay any longer and sent me to live with my granny. My granny is all I have. She looks after me more than my own parents. She cooks food for me and sends me to school." Tears rolled down Pastor Ramsey's cheeks for Jimmy's story had touched the depths of his soul. Removing the flower from his coat he told Jimmy, "This flower alone is not enough for your granny. Go to the front of the altar, take the bouquet you find there and present it to your granny." When Jimmy gave the bouquet to his granny and wished her 'Happy Birthday,' she warmly took his hand*

in hers and in a voice choked with emotion said, 'Of all the flowers you have brought for me, you my child, is the most beautiful!'

Love is said to be a "radioactive" power which can transform the whole world and lift any burden.

Anthony Castle *cites the following incident: V. Backman had enjoyed a picnic with his family at the beach. As he got his car ready for the trip home the scream of his four-year-old son sent him out of his automobile. He winced with fright when he saw what he had done. In backing up, he had run over his own boy. Without a pause, the 130-lb man grabbed the bumper of the 3,000-lb car and almost miraculously lifted it high enough to free the boy pinned under one of the wheels.*

Alice, mother of an eight-year-old girl was small, weak and sickly. She was the kind of person who makes you think: "If the wind blows too hard, she'll fly away." Her health had not been good for several years now, and it took her a great deal of effort to get through her normal day.

One day, her daughter who studied at the community school did not return as usual. Alice panicked and ran to the school in anxiety. Screams and shouts in a voice she recognised as her daughter's made her rush to her classroom only to find the door locked. She realised her daughter had been locked in. There was not a human in sight who could help. The child was getting more and more scared. What the frail mother did next was something none who know her would have thought her capable of. She caught hold of two of the iron bars in the window and bent them apart wide enough to allow the child to come out of the room! You have seen iron bars on windows. Bending them with one's bare hands is not something most of us can do, much less a physically weak person like Alice. What gave her such tremendous strength? Evidently, it was the love for her child.

When Mrs. Philomina's daughter was seriously ill, and admitted in the intensive care unit of a hospital, the authorities would only allow one person to stay with her. The only person she was really comfortable with was her mother. The only piece of furniture in the small cell, in addition to the patient's bed, was a stool. There was no cot or bench for the attendant to lie on. Philomina spent eight days and nights in that cell looking after her daughter, without ever lying down. She stood or sat, and went without sleep for eight full days and nights. She is a middle-aged woman who normally needs sleep and rest, like the rest of us. When the doctors asked her how she managed that, she said: "Looking back, I too do not know how I managed it. I suppose that, when there is real love, we somehow find the strength."

Love gave all the people in the illustrations above the strength to do things which medicine or their state of health would not have permitted under normal circumstances. Deep down inside, we are all aware of this immense reservoir of strength that we summon in extremely stressful situations when a loved one's life or welfare is at stake.

A fragile looking mother was carrying a small child on her back. The path climbed up into the mountain and the woman panted. A passerby said sympathetically: "You are carrying a heavy burden." The woman replied, "That's not a heavy burden. He's my son!"
(E.M. Kremer)

William Gladstone, *in announcing the death of Princess Alice to the House of Commons, told a touching story. The little daughter of the Princess was seriously ill with diphtheria. The doctors told the princess not to kiss her little daughter for in doing so she would be endangering her own life by breathing in the child's breath. Once when the child was struggling to breathe, the mother, forgetting herself entirely, took the little one into her arms to keep her from choking to death. Rasping and struggling for her life, the child said, "Momma, kiss me!" Without thinking of herself the mother tenderly kissed her daughter. She got diphtheria and some days thereafter she went to be forever with the Lord. Real love forgets self. Real love knows no danger. Real love doesn't count the cost!*

The opposite of being loved and accepted is being rejected — something we've all experienced at one time or another in our lives. Who among us has never felt embarrassment, humiliation, failure, fault, or someone's disapproval over something we've done? Whether it be by a family member, a friend, or a complete stranger, rejection happens to all of us.

> *A freelance reporter from* **The New York Times** *was interviewing* **Marilyn Monroe** *years ago. She was aware of Marilyn's past and the fact that during her early years Marilyn had been shuttled from one foster home to another. The reporter asked Marilyn, "Did you ever feel loved by any of those foster families with whom you lived?"*
>
> *"Once," Marilyn replied, "when I was about seven or eight. The woman I was living with was applying make-up, and I was watching her. She seemed to be in a happy mood, so she reached over and patted my cheeks with her rouge puff ... for that moment, I felt loved by her!"*

Marilyn Monroe had tears in her eyes when she remembered this event. Why? The touch lasted only a few seconds, and it happened years before. It was even done in a casual, playful way, not in an attempt to communicate great warmth or meaning. But as small as the act was, it was like pouring a bucket of love and security on the parched life of a little girl starved for affection.

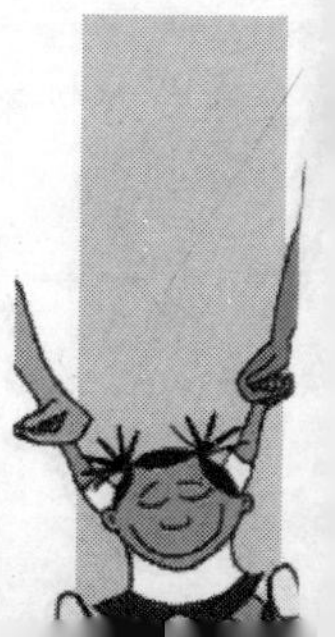

To love your children, you must remember

1. They are children
2. They tend to act like children
3. Much of childish behaviour is unpleasant
4. If you do my part as a parent and love them despite their childish behaviour, they will be able to mature and give up their childish ways
5. If you only love them when they please you (conditional love), and convey your love to them only during those times, they will not feel genuinely loved. This in turn will make them insecure, damage their self-image, and actually prevent them from moving on to better self-control and more mature behaviour. Therefore, their behaviour is your responsibility as much as it is theirs
6. If you love them unconditionally, they will feel good about themselves and be comfortable with themselves. They will then be able to control their anxiety and, in turn, their behaviour, as they grow into adulthood.

A young man was serving a sentence in jail when a priest came to visit him. Grieved to see him among hardcore criminals he put his hand on his shoulder and, with a loving look, asked him: "My friend, how is that you're here too?" The young man was deeply moved and, with tears in his eyes, replied in a low voice: "Father,

I wouldn't be here if someone had only put his hand on my shoulder like that before!"

"Love me when I least deserve it, that's when I really need it."

Harold Hulbert

IS YOUR TEEN TELLING THE TRUTH

DENISE WITMER

Even good teenagers, occasionally lie to parents for different reasons. They want their privacy, more freedom and feel they deserve to have it; they make mistakes that get them into trouble which they need to get out of by lying. While parents may take lying about these issues seriously, teens, on the other hand, do not think it is a big deal. It is a parent's responsibility to teach their teen that lying is a serious issue. But how can you tell if your teen is lying in the first place?

The faster you get over the shock that your teen will lie to you, the better you will be at spotting when (s)he is lying. Your teen will not be trying to hurt you by lying, so try not to get too emotional.

Here's how to spot when someone is lying:

When someone lies, they get defensive and will be upset if you try to check on their story. When a teen is not lying, (s)he will tell you how to check up by giving you the phone numbers or names you need. They may be a little insulted but they aren't defensive. Being defensive and throwing a fit when asked to help you check the story is a sure sign something is amiss.

If your teen avoids looking at you when telling you a story or looks at you too long without blinking, this is an indication that (s)he may be lying. People tend not to look you in the eye when lying, unless they know this fact and tend to look at you for too long. If you talk to your teen on a regular basis, you'll see a deviation in how (s)he behaves while talking to you during a lie.

Many times when a person lies, they look down. When a person tells you what happened and it's the truth, they tend to look up and 'see' the event happening as it did. But when someone is using their creativity to 'make up' what happened, they look down.

People who are lying touch their face and mouth. It isn't easy to pick up until you know to look for it.

There will be a pause before they answer a simple question to buy time to make something up.

People who are lying fidget. But this is also a sign of stress, so don't go by this alone. Ask to check up on the story.

Teens who are lying avoid details, or have them well practised, but the story is usually different the second time. This rarely happens with intelligent teens. Check up on the story and await reactions.

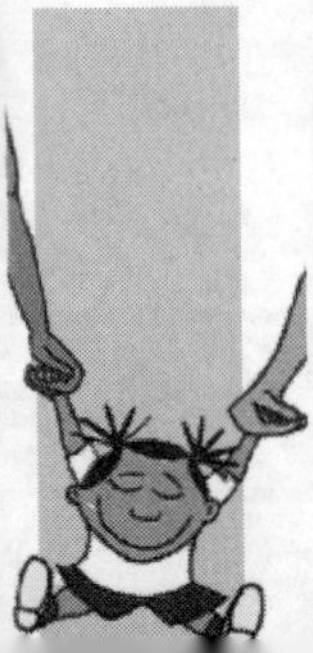

5

BEING A CHARACTER ROLE MODEL

"We are apt to forget that children watch examples better than they listen to preaching."

Clarence Budinton Kelland

CHAPTER FIVE

A man had a dream. He dreamt his teenage son was playing in an open field with a number of other kids his own age. Suddenly, without a warning, the young lad disappeared into a dark bylane. The man yelled out to him, "Son, where are you going?" as he moved farther away, the boy turned to his dad and said, "Dad! You never showed me the right path to follow."

The father suddenly woke up with a shock and took a good look at himself. He realised that he had not been an example for his son to emulate. The dream left such a profound effect on the father that he resolved to change his life.

One of the most powerful teaching tools parents have is modelling the behaviour they want children to learn. In character education, that means **"walking the talk,"** or being the person of high integrity you're helping your children to become.

You may be a great role model now, but remember, you don't have to be sick to get better. Everything you do, ***and don't do***, sends a message to your child about your values. Be sure your messages are about doing the right thing, even when it is hard to do. When you slip (and all of us do), act the way you want your children to behave when they make a mistake — be accountable, apologise sincerely and work to do better.

> ***Albert Schweitzer*** *was asked what advice he would give on being an effective parent. "I can give you three words of advice," he replied. "The first is 'example.' The second is 'example;' and the third is also ... 'example.'" By our example, we are teaching our kids constantly!*

Progressive parents teach their children by words as well as deeds. They talk about their values, share their expectations, and they teach right from wrong. Teaching with words is very important, but it is not enough by itself. When our words and actions are congruent, when what we do matches what we say, we are sending our children a very powerful message.

The following ***"Parents' Pledges"*** were developed by the **Character Counts Coalition** to help parents focus on specific behaviours they can model as part of their teaching. Perhaps they will be a source of inspiration for you.

A Parent's Pledge: Trustworthiness
I will be as honest as I want my children to be.
I won't lie to my children or in front of them.
I will not treat honesty as a rule of convenience by excusing acts of dishonesty or deception as exceptions.
I will avoid hypocrisy like preaching against smoking,
drinking or drugs while doing those activities.
I will demonstrate consistently the strength of

my moral convictions by paying whatever price necessary to do what I think is right, risking loss of money, approval and even employment.
I will treat my word as my bond in all cases.
I will avoid legalistic escape hatches in dealing with my children, honouring the spirit as well as the letter of my promises.

A Parent's Pledge: Respect
I will listen with respect and treat my children's views seriously.
I will avoid selfish and petty behaviour and power plays, especially where my children are concerned.
I will exercise self-restraint and maintain the kind of self-discipline I expect from my children with respect to violence, yelling or other displays of temper.
I will use only the kind of language I want my children to use.

A Parent's Pledge: Responsibility
I will demonstrate a willingness to admit when I am wrong and to take my medicine, and expect the same from my children.
I will avoid shifting the blame and making excuses regarding my own shortcomings or mistakes, and expect the same from my children.
I will assign reasonable age-appropriate responsibilities to my children and see that

there are meaningful consequences if they fail to perform their duties.
I will insist that my children keep their commitments at home, at school and in extracurricular activities.

A Parent's Pledge: Fairness
I will not resort to arbitrary power to get my way when I have taught that general rules of fairness are applicable.
I will treat all my children equally and fairly.
I will be open and reasonable to discussion.

A Parent's Pledge: Caring
I will remember that my children
are stakeholders in everything I do.
I will demonstrate compassion and respect for others,
especially my children.
I will be visibly charitable and involve my children
in choosing charities to support.
I will not discount, belittle or trivialise my children's feelings and fears.

A Parent's Pledge: Citizenship
I will obey the law in all matters.
I will vote in all elections and perform
other civic duties,
testifying as a witness and
reporting crimes as the opportunities arise.

I will conserve energy and avoid littering or other forms of pollution.

Children learn many things, good or bad, from parents. They observe the behavioural patterns of parents. Children are not much impressed with the tons of advice and preaching given by parents. The best gift that parents can offer their children is their own example of leading a pure and virtuous life.

This humorous anecdote serves to drive home the point as we bring this chapter to a close.

One day the boy asked his Dad: "Dad, did you go to Sunday School when you were a kid?"
Dad replied, "I sure did. Never missed a Sunday."
Then the boy turned to his mother and said, "See Mom, it won't do me any good either!"

"The really tough thing about being a parent is that you have to be the sort of person you want your children to become."

Myra Ellen Barbeau

SAVING YOUR CHILD FROM PEER PRESSURE

"No child is immune to peer pressure."

Kathi Hudson

CHAPTER SIX

From the first time (s)he plays with siblings or other children, your child is affected by peer pressure. There's no way you can possibly make peer pressure go away, but you ***can*** teach your child how to deal with it effectively. Typical forms of peer pressure is when kids the same age urge their friends to drink, do drugs, have sex, cheat on tests, gossip, agitate or ostracise less popular members of the group, among other things.

Young people are particularly susceptible to peer pressure due to insecurities, desire to fit in, looking for status, need for excitement, fear of losing friends, wanting to be noticed or envied, looking to assert autonomy, finding an identity, looking for support or approval and wanting to excel at something.

> *In Mumbai, a Higher Secondary student was hospitalised after swallowing 75 pills in a case of attempted suicide. The young woman later summed up her feelings, "It is a dictatorship of peers; you have to measure up to everyone's standards. It is either to conform or burn out."*

> *The other day, Richard, 12, went for a movie with 'A' certification because his friends had invited him. They said it was the craze of the town. Richard could not refuse because he was afraid his friends would think he was either too scared to break the law or too sissy!*

Your young child experiences social pressure every time (s)he is with people! Social pressure can be exerted or manifested in a number of ways, including...

- Verbal pressure from adults who criticise or challenge
- Physical pressure from bullies or siblings
- Expectation pressure from teachers or parents
- Social-judgement pressure from peer groups
- Self-pressure

Although we often think of peer pressure as bad, it is possible for your children's friends to influence them in positive ways. Just as an iron knife can sharpen the dull edge of another knife, fellowship with some youth can sharpen your personality and make you a better person — if those peers have mature, healthy attitudes.

Here are some ways you might find effective in helping your children resist negative peer pressure:

Develop a good relationship. The stronger your relationship is with your children, the less likely they are to follow bad examples.

Teach your children to think when others try to get them to do something. Your children should ask themselves questions like: Is it wrong? Why do they want me to do it? Is it illegal? Why am I tempted to go along? Am I afraid that they will laugh at me?

Teach your children to decide for themselves whether something is right or wrong, helpful or harmful. Bring up examples of situations they may be in; then explore what might happen if they respond a certain way. Let them think about the consequences of their actions. If they have an uneasy feeling, something is probably wrong.

Sometimes children just need help getting away from a bad situation. Provide them with some responses they can use to resist peer pressure. Encourage them to avoid giving an immediate 'Yes' or 'No' answer when friends want them to do something questionable. They can buy time to make a good decision by saying, 'Maybe later,' or 'I'll wait and see.' Let them use you as an excuse: "I'll be grounded forever if I try that!"

Practise situations with your children, trying various responses that they are comfortable saying. Let them play themselves and the peer when you practice. Ask your child what gives him or her trouble when faced with a tough decision, and incorporate that in the practice. Use it to help your children build confidence in their ability to say 'No!'

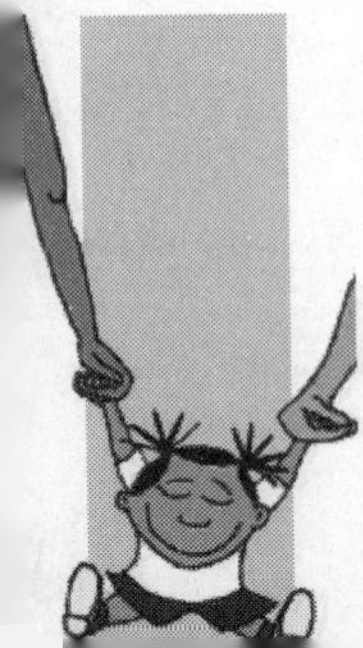

Teach your child to say 'No.' Abuse of dangerous drugs by children is widespread — not just marijuana, heroin and cocaine, but also alcohol, tobacco, anabolic steroids, and a variety of inhalants and stimulants, both prescription and over-the-counter stuff.

Kids are offered drugs at an alarmingly early age. That's why it is imperative that you talk to your children about the dangers of substance abuse while they're still young. If your child is offered drugs, how do you think (s)he would respond? Have you taught your child what to do in that type of situation?

Saying 'No' is a skill you need to teach your child. The best course of action is prevention. Teaching your children that they have the power to say 'No' is the first step. You must also be willing to talk often to your children about the dangers of drugs, keeping the communication lines open. Effective communication means that you're an active listener. Your children should know that they can talk to you about any subject, no matter how sensitive.

Here are five helpful hints you as a parent can use to help pressure-proof your children:

1. **Identify risk factors.** Keep your eyes and ears open and discover the types of social pressures that easily influence your child. Identify what and why your children are susceptible to peer pressure.

2. **Be protective.** Protect them by finding ways to lessen how much time they spend in unsupervised activities where sources of social pressure are present.

3. **Be a teacher.** Teach and empower your children with skills that will help them to deal with stressful/pressure-packed situations.

4. **Monitor and plan.** Design and implement appropriate ways for your children to get their needs *(to fit in, belong, excitement, etc.)* met. This might include maximising the time they spend with appropriate social influences.

5. **Communicate.** Talk with your child. Maintain strong relationships with your children that include open, honest communication.

"The ugly reality is that peer pressure reaches its greatest intensity at just the age when kids tend to be most insensitive and cruel."

Walt Mueller

DEVELOPING YOUR CHILD'S TALENTS

"Buried seeds may grow but buried talents never."

Roger Babson

CHAPTER SEVEN

John Powell says that every child sent into this world comes with a special message to deliver, with a special song to sing to others, with a special act of love to bestow. No one can speak his message, or sing his song, or offer his act of love.

It is the responsibility of every parent to identify and nurture the talents of their children. There is something very sad about seeing talent go to waste, for when talent goes abegging it is not the talent by itself but the person who wields it that also goes to waste. A brilliant footballer turns to drink, an exciting singer turns to drugs, a bright young politician is sucked into the system, a beautiful nurse loses her healing touch...and their talents are lost; perhaps forever!

How often have we heard people excuse themselves by using to what they do not have as a scapegoat! “I'm too old...”, “I'm too young...”, “I'm not educated...”, “I'm too busy...”, “I'm not good enough!” “I feel shy...”, “I feel nervous...” or “I could never do that!”

What do you mean by talent?

Talent is a natural ability to perform an activity extremely well. You probably know a great number of people in your social circle who are blessed with certain talents. Maybe they're really

good at playing the piano, draw exceptionally well or have an amazing voice. It's easy to tell because we can clearly see the talents in others.

To my mind, talent is everything you have and everything you are. This includes your abilities — to sing, to dance, to smile, to help, to lead to organise, to play, your material and financial resources; your relationships with loved ones and friends, in short, your very life!

Quite often we think that a talent has to be something 'tangible.' We've been conditioned to only think of talent as something we only see on stage, such as being a good singer, dancer, or piano player. Most of the time you'll find your talents to be something "intangible" such as getting along with people, or figuring out how things work and fixing them, or being able to clearly communicate your ideas across to people and so on.

Does everyone develop their talents?

Everyone is born with a talent for something or the other. Smart people use it. The University of Chicago did a five-year study of leading artists, athletes, and scholars. The research was conducted by **Dr. Benjamin Bloom**, and was based on anonymous interviews with the top 20 performers in various fields. These people included concert pianists, Olympic athletes,

tennis players, sculptors, mathematicians, physicians, and a number of other achievers. Bloom and his team of researchers from the University probed for clues as to how these people developed their skills. For a more complete picture, they even interviewed their families and teachers. The report stated conclusively that ***it was not great talent, but drive and determination that led to the extraordinary success of these individuals.*** Bloom noted, *"We expected to find tales of great natural gifts. We didn't find that at all. Their mothers often said it was another sibling who had the greater talent!"*

> *A plain bar of iron is worth US $5. The same bar made into a pair of horseshoes would be worth about US $50. Made into medical needles, it might be worth as much as US $5,000. And if it were made into balance springs for fine Swiss watches, that iron bar might bring in as much as US $500,000. Here's the point: Raw material must be developed. God has blessed each of us with gifts and talents. It all depends on how we develop our raw material.*

According to **William James**, human beings use only 10-12% of their potential. Isn't it a pity that many people drift through life, living aimlessly, selfishly, and foolishly, and die without having realised even a fraction of their potential? The saddest part of most people's lives is that they die with the music still in them.

How talent can ruin children?

Curious though it might sound, talent can ruin children if they are not careful. They can be carried away by their talent and become egotistic, immature and selfish.

Star footballer ***Paul Davis*** *did have to work hard at it as a youngster, still everyone agreed he was 'a natural.' He had it, and had it from the very beginning. It came as no surprise, therefore, when he was snapped up by a leading First Division Club at just age 15! He didn't have to wait long for his big chance. He had only just celebrated his 16th birthday when he found himself selected for the first team. He grabbed this opportunity and made an immediate impact retaining his place in the team. Almost overnight he shot from obscurity to fame.*

From there on it was one success after another. Within two years he was the club's leading scorer. By now he was also playing for his country. Wherever football was talked about, Paul's name was mentioned. To the fans he was a hero. To the media he was a celebrity. Many girls said, "If I have Paul, I have everything!" He married a beautiful model, drove a Mercedes, and was the envy of all.

Soon, though, the lights began to dim... too many friends, too many girls, too much money... There were rumours that he had taken to drinking — heavily! His football career began to dip. His personal life suffered. His wife left him. She claimed he was immature, selfish and irresponsible. Sadly, Paul's glittering career came to a premature end. Beware of talents that are born! Of what use is it to develop one's talent if one leaves oneself undeveloped?

Eve Lavalliere *was one of the most popular actresses in Paris in the early part of the 20th century. She was also a wonderful singer. One evening Eve outdid herself and earned a standing ovation and several bouquets. After the performance the spectators wanted to carry her triumphantly through Paris. But Eve managed to slip out without being seen. On his way home one of the spectators had to cross a bridge over the Seine and saw a woman on the verge of jumping into the river. He ran and reached her just in time. The woman burst into tears and then the man recognised her. It was Eve Lavalliere! "Why would you want to commit suicide – specially tonight after such a great triumph when everyone applauded you as the most beautiful woman in France?"*

"Triumph, glory, beauty," mumbled Eve, "What is it? Smoke, just smoke! But who can take away the anguish in my heart?"

This story tells us happiness is neither strength nor wealth; neither fame nor power. It is the proper use of talent.

How can a child identify his or her talents? It seems ironic that while we clearly seem to see talent in others, we cannot clearly see it in ourselves. It often takes somebody from the outside looking in to point them out to us. If you are a parent, friend or teacher, you have the responsibility of identifying what your children, or your friend, or your student's talents are. You should be the one to point out to them what they are naturally good at and encourage them to develop those talents; unless you point it out to them, they won't know it — not so much because they can't see it, but more because they are merely waiting for reaffirmation of their beliefs. Which brings us to the moot question: How does one identify skill and talent.

Asking yourself the following questions might prove helpful in identify your child's talent:

- Do they exhibit a knack for something?
- What are they always recognised for?
- What do they amaze others by doing?
- What can they do that most people struggle with?
- What do others tell them they are great at doing?

When you get some answers, take them through the following questions:

- Do they get into a 'flow' when engaging in that particular activity?

- Do they have a deep desire to become better at it?
- Do they admire people who engage in that activity and do it well?

Once you have identified the talent, you must encourage and foster the child in building up on it by giving him or her ample opportunity, guidance and motivation.

What are developed skills?

Skills learned via education, practice or experience — acquired skills — can be classified as developed skills. A simple example of a developed skill is typing. The child probably acquired it in school when he had to type up papers for class. By constantly typing he is likely to improve in speed and accuracy and by virtue of this fact could become a professional. Another example of a developed skill is cooking. The child may have gone to a culinary school and got experience in that field, resulting in developing its cooking skill.

Developed skills can also be the result of high interest in a particular hobby, subject, or field. For example, reading can be a developed skill if the child has a high enough interest in it. If (s)he's interested in reading, (s)he'll find enough material for reading and will be reading during free time and since (s)he does it often, (s)he becomes so much better at it that it turns into a skill naturally.

What are potential skills?

These skills are ones that haven't yet grown into full blown "developed skills," but have the potential of becoming a talent or a developed skill. These potential skills are often found seeded in subjects of high interest. If the child has a high enough interest in let's say chess, he plays it online frequently, plays it with friends, buys books on it, memorises strategies, and joins clubs among other things, chess for him has effectively become a developed skill over time.

Tell your children to seek within themselves and identify their own talents and develop them. They are their gifts. They are their superpowers so to speak. They can be found within each and every child. As parents, it is your responsibility to become aware of them in your child, develop them, and leverage them for their successful living.

"The real tragedy of life is not in being limited to one talent, but in the failure to use the one talent."

Edgar W. Work

Alcoholism is a substance-use disorder in which the sufferer has problems managing how much alcohol they drink, and their lives as a result. The symptoms of alcoholism include tolerance to alcohol, withdrawal episodes, using more alcohol for longer periods of time, and problems managing life issues due to alcohol.

IS YOUR CHILD A VICTIM OF JUVENILE ALCOHOLISM?

SUSAN TAPERT

Alcoholism is caused by a number of individual, family, genetic, and social factors rather than by any one cause.

What are the causes and risk factors of teen alcoholism?

Family risk factors for teenagers developing drinking problems include low parent supervision or communication, family conflicts, inconsistent or severe parental discipline, and a family history of alcohol or drug abuse. Individual risk factors include problems managing impulses, emotional instability, thrill-seeking behaviours, and perceiving the risk of using alcohol to be low. Girls who drink, as well as teens who begin drinking prior to the age of 14 years and those whose mothers have drinking problems, are more likely to develop alcoholism. Teen risk factors for alcoholism differ a bit between the 14 to 16-year-old and 16 to 18-year-old age groups, in that 16 to 18-year-olds tend to be less likely to drink in excess when they have a close relationship with their mothers.

How can I tell if my teen is drinking on the sly?

The most common symptoms of alcohol abuse in teenagers include lying, making excuses, breaking curfew, staying in their rooms, becoming verbally or physically abusive toward others, having items in their possession that are connected to alcohol use, the excessive use of deodorants or strongly scented chewables to mask the smell of alcohol on their body or breath, mood swings, stealing, and changes in friends.

Discussing the negative effects of alcohol, and expectations regarding drug (ab)use, have been found to significantly decrease alcohol abuse in teens. Alcohol, and other drug use, has been found to occur most often between the hours of 3 and 6 p.m., immediately after school and prior to parents' arrival at home from work. Teen participation in extracurricular activities has therefore been revealed to be an important measure in preventing use of alcohol in this age group.

HONING YOUR CHILD'S PROBLEM-SOLVING ABILITIES

"The solution to adult problems tomorrow depends in large measure upon how our children grow up today."

Margaret Mead

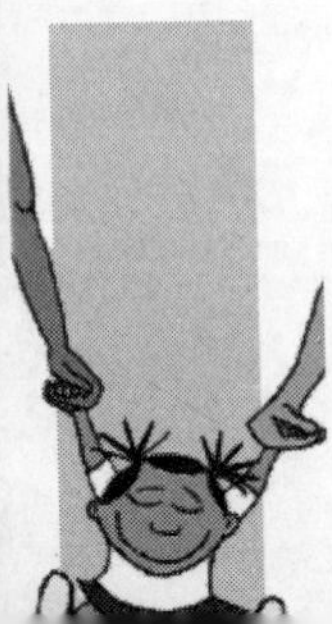

CHAPTER EIGHT

Problems are inevitable; good parents anticipate them. They accept the truth and face up to the reality of a situation and are not easily overwhelmed by emotion. But you can't let your problems be a problem.

Let's take the situation of an eight-year-old boy who had trouble sitting down to his homework. With daily arguments between them, his mother was at the end of her tether as to how to deal with the situation. This is what she did. Calling her son, she told him what they needed to do and both sat to note down solutions to the problem.

State the problem. You have a problem child at home. She is disobedient. She does not her home tasks on time. There are constant complaints about her from school. She looks moody and gets angry for silly reasons, etc. The first step is to acknowledge the problem.

Discuss the problem. Tell your child that you have noticed some change in her behaviour, something seems to troubling her or bothering her. Tell her of your love and your deep concern for her and your intention to help her. When she has regained her confidence in you, she will voluntarily come forward and discuss the matter with you.

Listen to the child's point of view. The mother asks the girl how she feels about the issue. She engages in **'active listening.'** Even if she disagrees with what she says, it is important that she accepts her feelings. When you actively listen to what your child is saying, you are giving her the message: ***"You are important to me."***

Brainstorm on possible solutions. Ask the child to propose certain solutions. The mother may add her own solutions.

Agree on a workable solution. From the list of alternatives, select the one which both of you agree upon. Commit to the solution for a defined time period, like a week or a fortnight or a month. As far as possible try to use your child's solutions.

Evaluate. At the end of the stipulated period decide whether the solution has worked or you need to go through the probable alternatives again.

> ***"If you want children to keep their feet on the ground, put some responsibility on their shoulders."***
>
> ***Abigail Van Buren***

MOTIVATING YOUR CHILDREN

"When a goal matters enough to a person, that person will find a way to accomplish what at first seemed impossible."

Nido Qubein

CHAPTER **NINE**

Motivation is what makes children do things. In another sense, it is something that makes them put real effort and energy into what they do. It is the will to act. In short, ***'Getting children to do willingly and well those things which have to be done.'***

Motivation is vital for all children if they are to give their best to it. Assuming that children are given the opportunity to perform well and have the necessary skills to achieve it, then effectiveness depends to a marked extent on the degree of their motivation.

The responsibility of motivating their children lies primarily with parents. It is they who are ideally suited to create an atmosphere conducive for the healthy growth and development of their children so that they may give of their best to both study and work.

> *Here is a story about a young boy who attended regular soccer practice but always sat in reserve and never made it to the playing eleven. Every day, during practice, his father would sit at the far end of the field, waiting for him to finish.*
>
> *The matches had started and for four days, he didn't show up for practice or the quarter or semi-finals. All of a sudden he showed up for*

the finals, went to the coach and said, "Coach, you've always kept me as a reserve and never let me play in the finals...today, please let me play." The coach said, "Son, I'm sorry, I can't let you. There are better players than you and besides, it **is** the finals, the reputation of the school is at stake and I cannot take such a big chance." The boy pleaded, "Coach, I promise I will not let you down. I beg you, please; let me play." The coach had never seen the boy plead like this before. He said, "Okay, son. Go, play. But remember, I am going against my better judgement and the reputation of the school is at stake. Don't let me down."

The game started and the boy played like a spirit possessed. Every time he got possession of the ball, he scored a goal. Needless to say, he was the best player and the star of the game. His team secured a spectacular win!

When the game finished, the coach went up to him and said, "Son, how could I have been so wrong about you. I've never seen you play like this before. What happened? What made you play so well?" The boy replied, "Coach, my father is watching me today." The coach turned around and looked at the place where he was used to seeing the boy's father sitting. There was no one there. He said, "Son, your father used to sit there when you came for practice, but I don't see anyone there today." The boy replied, "Coach, there is something I never told you. My father

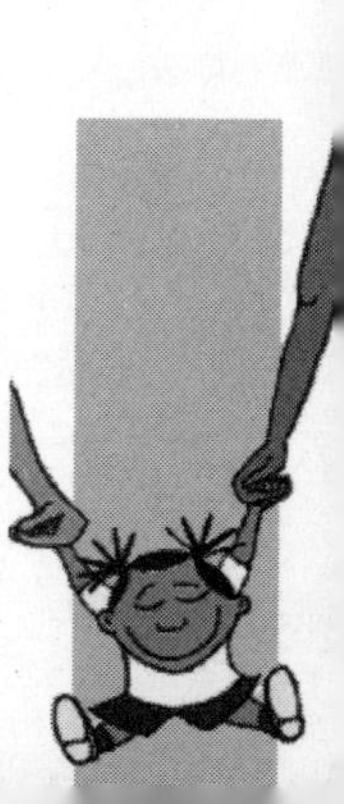

was blind. Just four days ago, he died. Today is the first day he is watching me from above!"

Listen to this parable about two friends, a mynah and an elephant. One day the elephant said: "You know, all my life I have wanted to fly. I have always dreamt of what fun it would be to fly over the village and look down at the houses and people, to glide over the river and jungle. Do you think I can fly?"

"Sure, you can" said the mynah. Reaching back with his beak, he pulled a feather from his tail. "Here," he said, "Take this feather and hold it firmly in your mouth. Then flap your ears as hard as you can and you will fly."

The elephant did as he was told. He put the feather in his mouth, flapped his ears as hard as he could and, lo and behold, he began to fly. Holding his feather tight in his mouth, he flew over the village. He looked down at the people, he glided over the river and over the trees. He did things he had never done, saw things he had never seen before. When at last he glided back to earth, he ran to meet his friend, guarding the feather carefully with his trunk. "Mynah, you've changed my whole life," he said, "I really can't thank you enough for this feather."

"That feather?" said the mynah, "You didn't need that. That was one of my old ones. I just gave you something to believe in. It was you that did it, not the feather!"

Motivation brings out the best in children and with it, even ordinary children can do extraordinary things.

The attitudes and behaviour of children very often reflect motivation or the lack of it. Examples of the signs of motivation are...

- Consistent high performance and good results
- Energy, enthusiasm, and determination to succeed
- Unstinting co-operation in overcoming problems
- Willingness and initiative in children to accept responsibility
- Children's openness to accommodate necessary change

Conversely, children who are demoralised or who lack motivation often display...

- Apathy and indifference to study and work
- Poor record of achievement and signs of lethargy
- Reluctance and refusal to obey and follow instructions
- Unjustified resistance to change

Motivate your children and you'll be surprised to see how fast they are capable of running!

TALKING TO YOUR PRETEEN ABOUT SEX

DENISE WITMER

It's never too early to start talking to your child about their body and their sexuality. However, the content and tenor of the talk need is different at different ages. **Here are some tips on talking about sex to preteens.**

Ensure your preteen knows the basics. If you haven't already explained to your preteen where babies come from, now is the time, as they most likely have heard it from their peers. You may need to see what information they have and then, give them the truth. Preteens are notorious for misinformation on sex.

Talk about body image and other issues. Adolescents are concerned with the way their bodies are starting to change. They will have concerns about what is and isn't normal. Let them know they are normal and everyone who has gone through this time has had the same valid concerns. Share some of the concerns **you** had when you were their age.

Discuss the consequences of sex. Preteens are learning about Newton's third law in science class at school: Every action has an equal and opposite reaction. Relate this to their lives in other ways. Some consequences can be wonderful when they happen at the 'right' age. Pregnancy is great at the right age but very hard at a young age. Share these feelings with your daughter as you discuss these issues.

Give your preteen every perspective. Give your preteen sexual information from both a woman's and a man's point of view. Moms can shed some light on what girls are all about to their son and Dads can impart an observation or two about boys to their daughter. If you feel uncomfortable — that's okay. Most likely, so does your preteen. Either keep these conversations light and witty, or clinical.

Tell your preteens that your door is always open for them. Most importantly, encourage your preteen to talk to you often about any questions they may have about sex. Remember that you are their person of choice when it comes to valuable life information. Your preteen does realise that they are facing choices and they will come to you with questions. Let them know that you will be there for them. Remember to bring up the fact that open communication with you about sex does not in any way imply that you condone sexual behaviour at their age or maturity. Saying this will clear any confusion your preteen may have and calm some of your own concerns.

THE IMPORTANCE OF DISCIPLINING YOUR CHILDREN

"Discipline your son in his early years while there is still hope. If you don't you will ruin his life."

Anonymous

CHAPTER TEN

Discipline, in its finest form, is ***"directing a child toward a better way."*** Discipline goes beyond punishment by instilling the desire never to repeat the misdeed, and instead, make a better choice. The desire to do right is born of love — the love of the child for the parent, and more importantly, the love of the parent shown to the child.

According to the *American Heritage Dictionary*, discipline is a type of training that is ***"expected to produce a specified character or pattern of behaviour" or "controlled behaviour resulting from such training"; but it can also be "punishment intended to correct or train."***

Discipline is loving firmness. It is direction. It is the pre-empting of a problem — anticipating and addressing it — before it arises. It is harnessing and channelling energy for great performance. Discipline is not something that you do ***to*** but ***for*** those you care about.

Parents must remember that discipline is an active love. Sometimes you have to be unkind to be kind: Not all medicine is sweet, not all surgery is painless, but we have to take it in our own best interests. We need to learn from nature.

> *We are all familiar with that big animal, the giraffe. A mama giraffe gives birth to a baby giraffe, standing. All of a sudden, the baby falls*

on a hard surface from the warm, secure sanctuary of the mother's womb, and sits on the ground. The first thing the mother giraffe does is to get behind the baby and give him a hard kick. The baby gets up, but his legs are weak and wobbly and the baby falls down. Mama goes behind again and gives him one more. The wobbly-limbed baby gets up but sits down again. Mama keeps kicking the baby till it gets on its feet and starts moving. Why? Because the mother knows that the only chance of survival for the baby in the jungle is to get it on its feet as soon as possible. Otherwise it will be killed by predators.

I have asked this question to a number of parents in my seminars: "If your child had a fever of 105°F and did not want to go to the doctor, what would you do?" Invariably they said they would get medical help even if the child resisted. Why? Because you are well aware that whether the child likes it or not, it is unlikely to survive unless urgent medical assistance is administered.

There is a popular misconception that freedom means doing your own thing. One cannot always have what one desires. Oftentimes it is not easy to comprehend the benefits of good values and discipline. It may even seem more profitable, enjoyable and convenient to do otherwise. There are countless instances where lack of discipline has prevented people from succeeding.

A boy was flying a kite with his father and asked him what kept the kite up. Dad replied, ‘The string.” The boy said, “Dad, it is the string that is holding the kite down.” The father asked his son to watch as he broke the string. Guess what happened to the kite? It came down.

Isn't that true in life. Sometimes the very things that we think are holding us down are the things that are helping us fly. That is what discipline is all about.

According to **George Washington**, “Discipline is the soul of an army. It makes small numbers formidable, procures success to the weak and esteem to all.” In the words of **J. Edgar Hoover,** “If discipline is practiced in every home, juvenile delinquency would be reduced by 95%.”

We hear this phrase all the time: “I want to be free!” If you take the train off the track, it is free, but where does it go? Ask yourself: Without discipline, Can a captain run a ship effectively? Can an athlete win a game? Can a violinist play well at a concert? The answer is, “Of course not.” Why then do we question today, in matters of personal conduct, or to achieve any standard, if discipline is necessary? It is absolutely necessary.

Today the philosophy is: “If it feels good, do it.” I have heard parents innocently saying, “I don't care what my kids do so long as it makes them happy. That's all that matters.” I ask them,

"Wouldn't you want to know what makes them happy?" If beating people up on the streets and taking their things away are what makes them happy, there is a word in the English language to describe them, it's called "Perversion."

Discipline means to do things in a controlled, orderly and regular way. A child who has been brought up in a disciplined way is quite different from a child who has been brought up to do whatever he wants.

Once upon a time there was a little boy, the only son of his parents, who was given everything he wanted. As an infant, he was given a toy gun as his first birthday gift. He was picked up, carried and held whenever he cried. His parents said, "He'll think we don't love him if we let him cry." He was never disciplined for leaving the home anytime. He was not required to get permission for anything from his parents. He suffered no consequences for breaking window panes or knocking down flowerpots. His parents said, "He'll think we don't love him if we stifle his will."

His mother did everything for him, made his bed, washed all his clothes and never allowed him to do any household work. His parents said, "He'll think we don't love him if we ask him to do chores."

Nobody ever stopped him from using bad words. He was never reprimanded for scribbling on his bedroom wall. His parents said, "He'll think we don't love him if we stifle his creativity."

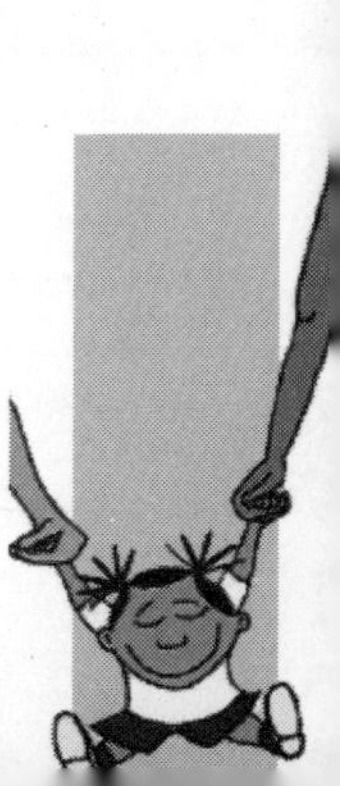

He never was required to go to religion class. He was never told about God and His creation. His parents said, "He'll think we don't love him if we force religion down his throat." One day the parents received news that their son was in jail on a criminal charge. They cried to each other, "All we ever did was love him and make sure that he never got hurt..." Unfortunately, that is, indeed, all they did.

A disciplined person is one who keeps regular hours for sleeping, eating and working. He keeps his room tidy and his things in an orderly manner. He has control over himself. He does not overeat, oversleep or lose his temper. He is not lazy. He does not waste his time. He is a person who can be relied upon.

A boy stole the instrument-box of one his school companions, and took it home to his mother. Instead of giving him a sound thrashing, she told him what a clever little chap he was.

When he grew up, he began to steal more valuable things, until one day he was caught in the act and sentenced to death. Among the crowd that lined the road to the place of execution was his mother, wailing and beating her breast. He sought permission from the gaoler and was allowed to whisper a word to her. He leaned down and drew her ear close to his lips; then he seized it between his teeth and bit it off. She screamed, and the crowd joined her in reproaching the unnatural son. "Goodness,"

they cried, "To end up by doing such a thing to his mother, even as he goes to the gallows, it is as if his wicked past is not enough!" The boy replied to them, "She's been the ruin of me. If she had given me the stick when I stole that instrument-box, I'd never have stood where I stand today."

According to the Bible, ***"No discipline seems pleasant at the time, but painful. Later on, however, it produces a harvest of righteousness and peace for those who have been trained by it."* (Hebrews 12:11)**

Recently, in an amusement park, I saw a large tree that had grown somewhat crooked. The oddest thing about the tree was that someone had placed an upright pole near it and tied it to the tree with ropes. But the tree had grown out so far from the place where the trunk came out of the ground that there was a lot of distance between the pole and the tree. It was too late for the pole to be of any help to the tree.

This often happens in the raising of children when parents allow them to run wild for the first 15 years of their lives. When the parents realise their mistake and try to correct or straighten out their children, they find it's too late to make any difference without intervention from an outside source.

Children require regular and consistent discipline. It creates limits and shows them that someone cares enough about them to set them on the right path. It is also a part of a loving relationship with your children and is necessary in helping them become responsible adults.

The Five 'C's of Effective Discipline

Children who are most at risk of using alcohol and other intoxicating substances come from homes where discipline is inconsistent, too harsh or lacking altogether. You can reduce the risk by following the 5 'C's of effective discipline with your children:

1. **CLARITY:** Be clear when you set rights, rules and limits.
   - o Don't assume your children know family rules until you've talked about them
   - o Be sure your children understand why these rules are being made and the consequences of breaking them
   - o Involve your children as far as possible in rule making
   - o Try writing out your family rules and posting them on the refrigerator door

2. **CONSISTENCY:** Be consistent when with rules.
   - o Stick to the consequence that has been established for a broken rule

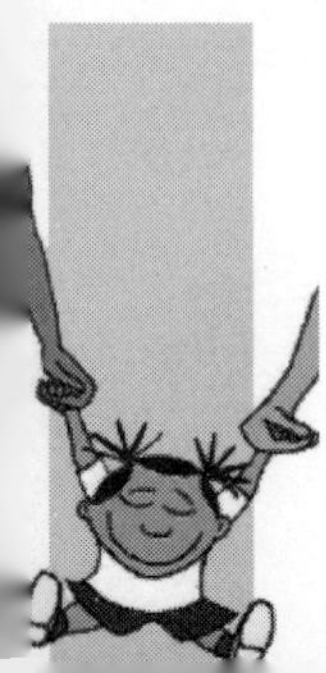

- o Discipline will be more effective if your children have been involved in establishing the rules
- o If a change needs to be made in a family rule, talk about it before the rule is broken
- o Be flexible — as your children grow, they're ready for expanded rights and changes in rules and limits

3. **COMMUNICATION:** Talk about rights, rules and limits often.
   - o Be willing to discuss the fairness of a rule and the reasons for it
   - o Help your children learn to talk with you about their feelings and even yours if need be
   - o Encourage your children to come to you when they need help, advice or simply a patient ear
   - o Express respect and faith in your child through your words, gestures and tone of voice.

4. **CARING:** Use encouragement and support, not just discipline for broken rules.
   - o Praise your children when they follow your family rules, especially when they do what's expected of them without reminders from you on earlier precedents
   - o When a rule is broken, criticise the action; not the children that broke the rule

- o Follow up swiftly when a rule is broken; stay calm and carry out the consequences your children expect
- o Make sure the severity of the consequences are commensurate with the magnitude of the broken rule
- o Respect your children's rights, such as the right to privacy

5. **CREATE:** Instil a sense of social responsibility in your children.
   - o Let your children know you expect moral behaviour, like honesty and fairness
   - o Set an example of honesty, fairness and social responsibility for your children to follow
   - o Promote your child's sense of self-respect

"Discipline is demanded of the athlete to win a game. Discipline is required for the captain running his ship. Discipline is needed for the pianist to practice for the concert. . . if parents believe standards are necessary, then discipline certainly is needed to attain them."

Gladys Brooks

LISTENING TO YOUR CHILDREN

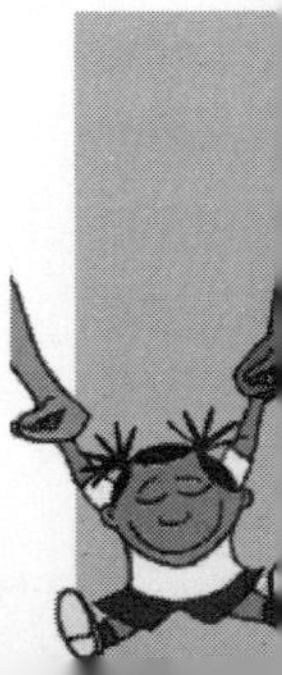

"The first duty of love is to listen."

Paul Tillich

CHAPTER **ELEVEN**

How often do you sit down and really listen to your children? Not simply ***hear***, but really ***listen***? Parents can sometimes settle into a pattern of teaching and directing, one-way communication. As difficult as it is to do sometimes, listening can reap invaluable rewards. Develop good listening skills when your children are very young, and continue to listen throughout your relationship with them.

Busy parents can get so focussed on daily responsibilities, they may miss festering problems or trends in their children's behaviour, especially as their children get older. Younger children share information more willingly and are not as complex in their communications or problems, and because younger children are more physically vulnerable, parents spend more time listening to them. This is a mistake. Teenagers are like toddlers, experimenting and getting burned. They, too, need comfort and guidance despite the fact they don't ask. Listening skills become more important as your children age, in part because you do not spend as much time with them as before. Listening to your older children is your primary source of feedback about how they're doing, what they're doing and, most importantly, who they're doing it with.

Recently on television, a public speaker was giving a talk about the three deepest needs of a child. What would you imagine those to be? The

> *first need children have, the speaker said, is to know someone who will listen to them. They all have a story to tell, a need to verbalise their feelings. They want someone who will listen to that. Secondly, he claimed, children want that the person listening to believe what they are saying. They want someone who will trust their story. Finally, the television speaker said that once they had found such a person who listened to them and trusted them, they wanted to be assured that such a person was on their side. They didn't want to be involved with someone who would misuse or abuse their story (through gossip, for instance), but would remain on their side, perhaps despite their story.*

Who can meet these needs of the children better than their own parents? But in this hyperactive, zip-drive world, most of the parents ***"don't have time"*** to sit and talk with their children much less **listen** to them. Their schedules are jam-packed. The more and better you listen, the more and better your children will like you, trust you and want to be close to you.

Listening to your kids is one of the main ways you can help them. Learn to really listen. When you ask, "How was school?" stop and listen to how their day went. When problems are presented to you, you don't always have to comment on the spot. Rather than pass judgement, take time to think about it, or pray for a solution. The main

thing is to be a listener; provide a listening ear, as well as love, encouragement and support.

Some teens were asked, "How do you know when your parents aren't listening to you?" They came up with the following answers: "If they're not looking at me." "If they're reading the newspaper while I'm talking." "If they keep vacuuming or cooking and say, 'Go ahead, I can hear you.'"

Cassidy, 18 makes this comment: "There's a difference between listening and really hearing. My parents hardly hear anything of what I am trying to say." Anna, 14, says, "My parents talk about how I am supposed to be slow to speak and quick to listen, but then they do just the opposite."

You can show you care by simply taking time to listen without judging and without advice. This short poem captures how badly people just want to be listened to.

PLEASE LISTEN
When I ask you to listen to me
And you start giving me advice,
You have not done what I asked.
When I ask you to listen to me
And you begin to tell me why
I shouldn't feel that way,
You are trampling on my feelings.
When I ask you to listen to me

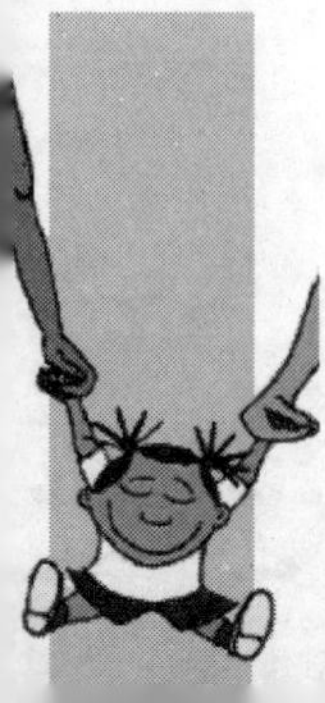

And you feel you have to do something
To solve my problem,
You have failed me,
Strange as that may seem.
Listen! All I ask is that you listen.
Don't talk or do — just hear me.

Guidelines on Listening to your Children

Be interested and attentive. Children can tell whether they have a parent's interest and attention by the way the parent replies or doesn't. Forget about the telephone and other distractions. Maintain eye contact to show you really are with the child.

Encourage talking. Some children need an invitation to start talking. You might begin with, "Tell me about your day at school." Children are more likely to share their ideas and feelings when others think them important.

Listen patiently. People think faster than they speak. With limited vocabulary and experience in talking, children often take longer than adults to find the right word. Listen as though you have plenty of time.

Hear children out. Avoid cutting children off before they have finished speaking. It is easy to form an opinion or reject children's views

before they finish what they have to say. It may be difficult to listen respectfully and not correct misconceptions, but respect their right to have and express their opinions.

Listen to non-verbal messages. Many messages children send are communicated non-verbally by their tone of voice, their facial expressions, their energy level, their posture, or changes in their behaviour patterns. You can often tell more from the way a child says something than from what is said. When a child comes in obviously upset, be sure to find a quiet time then or sometime that day to help explore those feelings.

Reflect feelings. One of the most important skills good listeners have is the ability to put themselves in the shoes of others or empathise with the speaker by attempting to understand his or her thoughts and feelings. As a parent, try to mirror your children's feelings by repeating them. You might reflect a child's feelings by commenting, *"It sounds as if you're angry at your math teacher."* Restating or rephrasing what children have said is useful when they are experiencing powerful emotions that they may not be fully aware of.

Show your appreciation. Let your child know you appreciate the fact that (s)he is sharing. Sometimes you may get confused by what

your child is trying to say, or maybe (s)he's saying one thing, but the body language is saying another. Try enlisting some of these clarifying phrases when this occurs:

"I'm not sure what you mean — tell me more."
"Can you give me an example of that?"
"Why do you feel this is best?"

Continue to ask short, brief questions until you understand what is being said. A great way to learn about what is going on with your teenager is to carefully listen to him or her. Although it sounds easy to just listen, effective listening can be a very active process. When teenagers feel that they are really being listened to, they are more likely to communicate their thoughts and feelings.

One of the hardest things about active listening is stopping yourself from trying to solve your kids' problems for them. Giving advice, talking about what you did in a similar situation, or sympathising are all ways parents try to help their kids. But when you just listen you're giving your kids the message that you trust them to solve their own problems.

All those who have the gift of sight can see, but every time they see, they may not observe the objects and persons around them. Anyone who has the power of hearing can listen, but it does not follow that he absorbs all he hears.

A group of young men were waiting to be interviewed for the job of wireless operator. They were talking among themselves and paid little attention to anything else. Just then another young man entered the room. He immediately listened to the stacatto barking da-da-did-da-da sound, that was coming over the loudspeaker outside the interviewer's room. He went into the office and after a few minutes, came out smiling.

One of the men waiting outside, called out, "How did you manage to get in ahead of us? We've been waiting here for hours!"

The young man grinned as he replied, "Any one of you could have got the job, if only you had cared to listen to the announcement that came over the loudspeaker in Morse code."

"What announcement?" they countered.

"The one that said: The first applicant that listens to this announcement and walks into the office gets the job."

The story above explains the importance of listening. Like those interviewees, most parents go through life only hearing but rarely listening to what their children are saying to them.

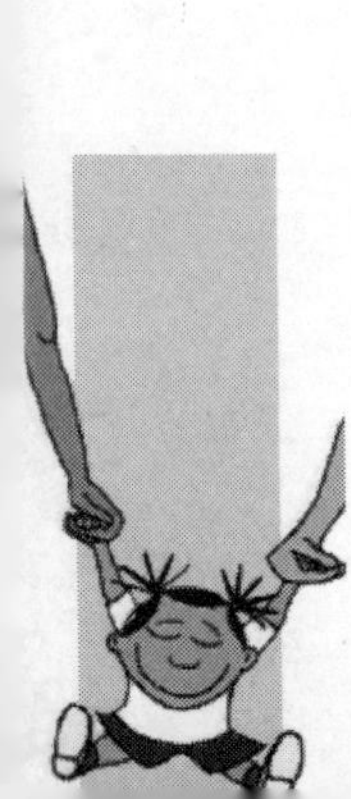

The teacher asked Jennifer to read a paragraph from her English textbook. Jennifer obeyed. The teacher then asked her to explain in her own words what the paragraph meant. Jennifer replied, "I'm sorry, sir. I was not listening."

In one of the Family Circus cartoon strips, the little girl looks up at her father, who is reading the newspaper, and says: ***"Daddy, you have to listen to me with your eyes as well as your ears."***

"Listen to the desires of your children. Encourage them and then give them the autonomy to make their own decision."

Denis Waitley

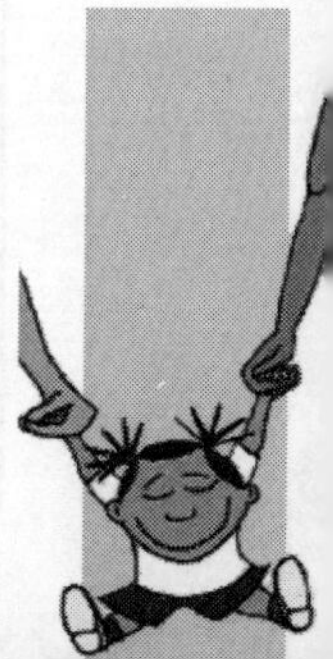

SHOULD YOUR KID HAVE A CELL?

WAYNE PARKER

If you are the parent of a teen or pre-teen, you will surely have heard the inevitable plea, "Can I get a mobile phone?" A third of urban teens or pre-teens carry a cell phone, and about 25% of all cell phone revenues come from this age group. It's not surprising that your child might feel left out if he or she doesn't have one. But while teens love them, moms and dads can get burned by cell phones in the hands of teenagers. Charges for excess minutes, for text messages, for phone-based e-mail and other services can be burdensome. A cell phone can also tend to change relationships (positive or negative) and can lead to some "dangerous liaisons." So, what should progressive parents know about teens and cells and what should they do to make the experience positive?

With an ever-growing market for the sale of cell phone services to teens, various cellular operators have a wide variety of choices to meet the needs of this segment of their market.

Currently, the plans tend to revolve around a few general choices. In a stand-alone plan, for example, your teen has a cell phone on his or her own account and receives a bill for that service. Generally, the plan includes a limited number of airtime minutes and a per-minute cost when the account uses more than the limited minutes. But the decision must largely be whether a parent wants his children to have a pre-paid or post-paid plan. Some service providers offer unlimited calls to a select few numbers. This can be helpful since members of the family can keep in touch easily without worrying about running up a huge bill. The key question in selecting a plan is how the phone will likely be used. For teens who can be irresponsible about the amount of time they spend on the telephone, a prepaid plan is a better idea. They can be given a certain allowance in a month and recharge their cards to that extent. Not only will this ensure that they do not spend too much time, talking or texting on the phone, it will teach them to be frugal in their spending. Since most handsets today come with a wide range of addons, including MP3 players, cameras and gaming devices, try and convince your child a simple phone is the best. While your teen does run the risk of being branded as old fashioned by his peers, it will significantly regulate the time (s)he spends on the phone!

11

GROOMING YOUR CHILD IN BEHAVIOUR AND MANNERS

"Good manners and soft words have brought many a difficult thing to pass."

John Vanbrugh

CHAPTER **TWELVE**

We are familiar with the phrase, *"Manners maketh the boy or girl"* by **William of Wykeham**. What this means is that a person is often judged by his manners. A well-bred child has good manners. An ill-bred child is ill-mannered. A miser, a thief, a gentleman, a selfish person and a proud man will all show the kind of people they are by their manners. To have good manners means to do things the right way, to behave properly and to talk politely. It is by politeness, etiquette and charity that society is saved from falling into a heap of savagery. If you want your child to demonstrate good etiquette, you must lead by showing. If you expect your child to say 'Please,' write 'Thank you' notes and be courteous to others, you need to do the same. Experts agree that when it comes to teaching good etiquettes, the best education happens at home.

Jeremy and his friends were watching ***Titanic*** *in a packed theatre. They were all set to enjoy the fascinating drama about to unfold on screen; but their enjoyment was short-lived. No sooner had the movie begun; a bunch of noisy latecomers entered the hall and occupied the empty front seats. They talked loudly, guffawed for no apparent reason and created so much commotion that the dialogue was rendered inaudible. As if all that was already not enough they even started flashing laser beams with*

unsavoury pictures and messages on the screen. It was, as if they had come to the movie hall with the sole purpose of disturbing the audience. Jeremy politely requested them to remain quiet, but this only seemed to spur them into making even more noise.

Such situations are all too familiar. We have all encountered noisy groups in cinema halls whose non-stop prattle, irritating giggling or popcorn munching can grate on the nerves. Equally annoying is the sound of a mobile phone ringing in the middle of a concert or seminar. It really makes one wonder why, despite repeated announcements, people still fail to switch the offending instrument off. We also meet people in public places who, oblivious to 'No Smoking' signs around them furiously puff away at their cigarettes forcing those around them to inhale the noxious fumes.

We have all witnessed motorists, pedestrians, picnickers, and beach-goers, blatantly going about littering public places — even though there may be a convenient trash can lying within a walking distance. In schools, students throw used tissues, empty cans of beverage, candy wrappers, chewing gums and an assortment of stuff all over the campus.

This type of outlandish behaviour could be attributed to poor upbringing and lack of parental education. Etiquette basically involves consideration and thoughtfulness. There's more to being well mannered than simply saying 'Thank you' or 'Please' — although these are equally important — or using the right fork at the table. It goes much further than that. Etiquette and social success go hand in hand. It helps to know the appropriate manner of conducting oneself in a variety of situations for it can only make a good impression thereby giving you a greater sense of self-confidence in the social milieu. Good manners contribute majorly in winning friends and influencing people. More importantly, they also help make a better human being out of a good one.

Looking for a job is difficult enough, the task becomes impossible if you do not possess the basic ingredients of geniality, politeness and a certain polish. Many employment-seekers, despite exceptional qualifications; fail to land the jobs they seek simply because their conduct fails to impress. If they do end up getting them, their career graphs either do not rise sharply or go into a downslide as they fail to gain popularity.

Good manners are lubricants that help quick locomotion with the same effect that oil has on wheels, or air on tyres. They make life smooth and pleasant. Good manners teach us to travel on the noble road of culture and refinement. Thinking well of all we encounter, using tact and diplomacy in speaking of others and doing good are the ingredients for making the perfect gentleman or lady.

Personal Etiquette

Teach your children good personal hygiene. Attention to body cleanliness and especially of the mouth needs no emphasis. Cleanliness is next to godliness. Those who are well-mannered know that certain things are to be done strictly privately. Natural functions like belching, yawning, sneezing and coughing and clearing of throat and nose should be done as silently as possible with an *'Excuse me,'* if in company. Sharing a room and bathroom and compartment with others imposes special obligations. A golden rule is always to leave things as you would like to find them left for you.

Good, neat and well-ironed clothes are important. These could include a good dark suit and perhaps a blazer and coordinated trousers (you can alternate them if you are called for more than one meeting). A couple of ties and good shirts add to the impression that you will make. Ladies can get away with a great deal more, but sarees and salwar suits that are not flashy are appropriate. Personal jewellery should be kept minimal.

Social Etiquette

Make sure your kids learn to address their elders by saying "yes sir" "no sir" "yes ma'am" and "no ma'am." It is better to explain to your child what sort of behaviour you expect from him before taking him out to a public place. It is usually futile

to glare or shout at him in front of others, especially if the child is throwing a tantrum. It only makes him more rebellious. It is even more embarrassing for you if your child refuses to listen to you. If you make your child recall the promises made at home, they usually try to keep them.

A person is expected to rise when ladies or their seniors enter a room. While introducing people, the following order is followed: Gentlemen are introduced to ladies, juniors to seniors, and young persons to old, with the exception in the case of VIP's to whom others are always introduced. The persons making the introduction should say some such words as "May I introduce..." or "Let me introduce Mr..." Shaking hands on being introduced is quite normal but not with ladies unless they make the first move.

> *A pompous young man lost his silk handkerchief and accused his neighbour of stealing it. After some confusion, the man found the handkerchief in his own pocket and apologised for having accused his neighbour. "Never mind at all," said the latter, "You thought I was a thief and I thought you were a gentleman, and we were both mistaken."*

A man can never be a true gentleman in manners until he is a true gentleman at heart. To be considered a gentleman, you need to speak gently and kindly, have an attractive and magnetic personality, refrain from evil, be unselfish and always be ready to serve, slow to judge and quick to forgive.

Table Manners

Manners and etiquette are revealed most at your dinner table. Here you are in everybody's view and are under active observation. Good table manners not only make you feel comfortable and look graceful at the table but also reflect your good breeding and refinement.

Here are some useful tips:

1. Make sure your clothes are appropriate for the occasion
2. The napkin should not be used as a towel
3. Do not drink tea or coffee from the saucer
4. Before helping yourself, offer the dishes to the people sitting on either side of you
5. Do not heap your plate, scrape or bang it
6. While eating, use appropriate cutlery for different dishes
7. Do not open the mouth wide long before the food is near it
8. Never talk with your mouth full and never talk loudly and don't over-stuff your mouth
9. It's considered courteous to thank your host for the wonderful lunch or dinner at the end

Manners in Conversation

Etiquette and manners also need to be followed in our day-to-day conversation with others. Fine vocabulary, a bit of wit and a good sense of humour can make the conversation lively.

Here are some don'ts:

1. Never attempt to dominate over a conversation, listen to others;
2. Never try to slander other's character and acts
3. Avoid the frequent usage of 'I', say 'We' instead
4. Don't be sarcastic to the other person or swear
5. Never comment on other's sense of dress, style or eating, etc.
6. Do not boast of either your attainments or your connections
7. Avoid personal queries about family and income
8. Never talk with hands in your pockets or on your hips or with a cigarette dangling from your lip

Thumb Rules of General Behaviour

- ❑ Be considerate and ready to help all, especially the aged, the sick and infirm and women
- ❑ Ladies should always get preference. Open the doors for them. Offer them seats
- ❑ When a person senior to you enters, rise from your seat. Do not argue, contradict or air your views boisterously

- ❑ Respect people and their peculiarities in dress, manners and customs
- ❑ Do not be rude because a person is poor or shabbily dressed or has a poor accent or appearance. Do not mimic them or make fun of them
- ❑ Do not hurt people with crude jokes or by making fun of their physical traits
- ❑ Whenever you make a mistake, remember to tender a sincere apology

Respecting Others' Privacy

It is wrong to read someone else's diary, personal letters, to listen in to a conversation between people on the telephone, to eavesdrop when people are speaking, to peep into a house through the windows or ventilators or into a room through the keyholes; to enter someone's room without knocking, or to search for things in their absence, to ruffle through others' desks, files, papers or belongings; to access others' mails or explore the content of their computers, to pry information from a person's lawyer, counsellor, doctor, psychologist, priest, etc.

Children who grow up without learning respect and tolerance, as well as how to act in social settings, are at greater risk of not being successful as adults in work settings and at social events. It is therefore the responsibility of every parent to start teaching and reinforcing appropriate

manners to their child right from their young age, so that their children will know what behaviour is expected of them in every circumstance.

> ***"We must become the change we wish to see in the world."***
>
> ***Mahatma Gandhi***

IT'S NEVER TOO LATE TO START AFRESH

"What the caterpillar calls the end of the World, the butterfly calls the beginning!"

Anonymous

IN CONCLUSION

Alfred Nobel, the famous inventor, woke up one morning to read his own obituary in the local newspaper. It said, *"Alfred Nobel, the inventor of dynamite, who died yesterday, devised a way for more people to be killed in a war than ever before, and he died a very rich man."*

Actually, Nobel's older brother was the one who had died, but the experience of seeing how he would have been remembered significantly impacted Nobel. He was grieved that if he had actually been the one to have died that day, he would have been remembered for figuring out an efficient way of killing large numbers of people, and amassing a fortune in doing so.

So deeply was he influenced by that one chance incident that he resolved to institute the Nobel Prize — the award for those whose contributions to society confer the greatest benefit on mankind. Nobel said, *"Every man ought to have the chance to correct his epitaph in midstream and write a new one."*

That, dear parent, is the take-away. It's never too late to start over. If you realise that you have not been the right kind of parent for your children, you can take heart in the fact that it's never too late to start afresh. You can take comfort in this book and implement the strategies contained in it

PRIVILEGE
AND
RESPONSIBILITY
OF PARENTS

and build healthy and warm memories for you and your children.

I know of a father who had more or less "iced" his kids out of his life. He immersed himself in his work and showed his love to his kids by buying them things, rather than by being there for them. At first the kids enjoyed the trinkets and baubles, but over time they grew to resent their father. They even grew to resent the very things they once thought were so cool! They tried to talk to Dad — but he wouldn't listen to what they had to say. Instead, he just became defensive and accused them of being ungrateful and spoiled. After a while, they stopped saying anything to him at all.

Over a period of a few years — perhaps as a result of Mom's prayers — Dad began to feel uncomfortable with the predicament. One night he said to the family, *"I've blown it. I'm sorry. Will you forgive me? Will you help me be the kind of husband and father that I should have been all along?"*

On hearing this, the children were thrilled! It was as if their Dad had 'come home.' They threw their arms around him and welcomed him back! In fact, this continues to be one of their most precious 'pictures' in their family scrapbook of memories.

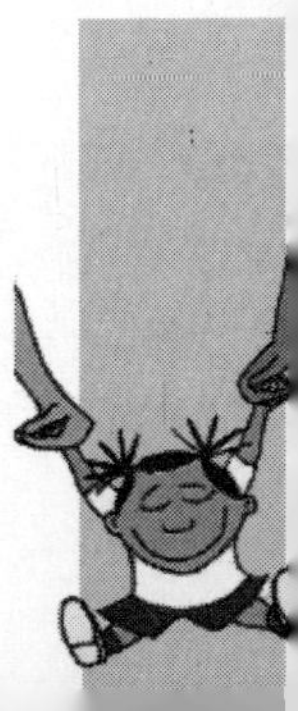

As your own family scrapbook continues to unfold, do all you can to make sure the pages are filled with love, joy, and warm memories. If you haven't been this way so far, simply turn the page and start afresh. Time has a way softening even the stoniest of hearts. Your job is to hang in there and be the best parent you can be. According to **Leo Buscaglia,** *"...a touch, a smile, a kind word, a listening ear, an honest compliment, or the smallest act of caring have the potential to turn a life around."*

Finally, when pages get ripped or torn — as they sometimes will — glue them back together again with love and tenderness, knowing your efforts are not in vain. If you do, one day you'll likely have an adult child look you in the eyes and say some of the most beautiful words a parent will ever hear: *"Thanks, Mom and Dad, for loving me when I was unlovable. I'll never forget it."*

Raising children, as we have seen, isn't for the fainthearted. It's a wild, exciting, and often chaotic adventure! But it's so worth it! So, hang in there, and keep on keeping on!

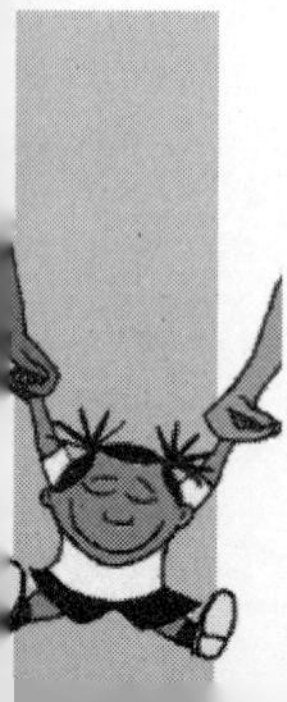

PART II

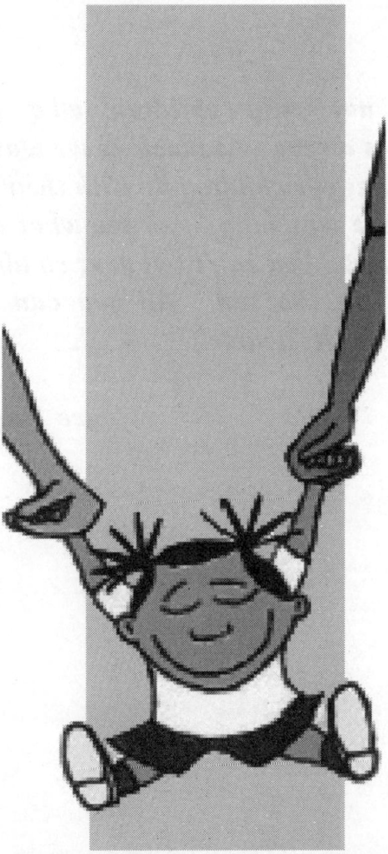

EXPERTSPEAK

"It's not only children who grow. Parents do too. As much as we watch to see what our children do with their lives, they are watching us to see what we do with ours. You can't tell your children to reach for the sun. All you can do is reach for it, yourself!"

Joyce Maynard

The Six Stages of Parenthood

From the **The Six Stages of Parenthood**
by child development expert ***Ellen Galinsky***

In her interviews with over 200 parents, Galinsky found that parents have "images" (visual expectations) about how things are supposed to go and the way they and their children are supposed to act. Usually, parents are not aware they have these expectations or that they judge their behaviour and their child's behaviour by these images. But even when these images are unconscious, we use them to measure our successes or failures as parents. If our behaviour or our child's behaviour doesn't match the image, then we may see this as a loss and feel angry and depressed. If the image and the behaviour are the same, then we feel happy and successful.

These parenthood stages occur when parents modify or change an image to be closer to the real behaviour, or they change the behaviour to more closely match the image. The parenthood journey is a personal story of ***"images failed and achieved."*** The stages are times when we put much of our energy into sorting our images of what we think should happen and what is really happening. Let's look at each of the stages more closely.

DOS
DON'TS

The first stage is the **Image-Making Stage.** It occurs during pregnancy. This is the time when parents think and form images about their new baby, what they will be like as parents, how the baby is going to affect their lives and the changes they will have to make.

The second stage, the **Nurturing Stage,** starts at birth and lasts until the baby is 18 months to 2 years — the age when 'No' is your baby's most important word. At this stage, parents compare their images of birth, of their child, and of themselves as parents with their actual experience.

The third stage is the **Authority Stage.** It starts at about the baby's second birthday and goes on until the child is 4 or 5. In this stage, parents have to decide how strict or permissive to be, what kind of rules they need and how to set them, and what to do when the rules are broken.

The fourth or **Interpretive Stage** begins about the time the child enters preschool or school and ends with the start of adolescence — about 11 or 12. In this stage, parents are concerned about how realistic they have been as parents and how they are helping their child develop positive self-concepts. They may worry about how to answer their child's questions and what kind of values, knowledge and skills they want their child to have.

The **Independent Stage**, the fifth in this series of progression is very similar to the Authority Stage but covers the child's teenage years. Parents have the same questions about rules, strictness and permissiveness, but now need different answers. As their child grows to adulthood, parents also need to start forming a different kind of relationship with their child.

The sixth and last stage is the **Departure Stage** — the time when the child leaves home. This is a stage of evaluation and, often, loss for the parents. Parents judge how well they have done and how their image of their child fits the reality. In addition, parents have to change their lives to let go of their child, to let their child become another adult.

Successful Parenting Begins with You

Zig Ziglar

Parenting can be a delight if you approach it with an open heart and mind. The following points may seem like basic common sense to you, but many people are so rushed by the pressures of making a living that they don't give much thought to these issues. They wrongly assume that rearing children just happens — they are born, they go to school, they leave home. If only life were so simple!

If you do these things, you'll realise what a joy parenting can be:

1. **Show unconditional love.** The most important step in successful parenting is to love your children unconditionally. You do not love your children because they are handsome or beautiful, are pleasant and courteous, consistently bring home 'A's, pick up after themselves, or for anything else that they do. If you put a condition on your love for them, they will always wonder if they have earned or deserve your love. This wonder breeds insecurity within children, and it ensures difficult times ahead.

2. **Accept that you are a role model.** A role model, in simple terms, is an individual whose

behaviour in a particular role is imitated by others. It is a parent's responsibility, like it or not, to demonstrate such noble qualities as courage, compassion, and genuine concern for others.

3. **Remember that your kids are not a responsibility that you handle at your convenience.** They are part of your schedule and can bring infinite joy or considerable misery. Much of that is determined by the time and effort that you put into raising your kids. An hour at the end of a hectic day is not quite enough to get the job done, especially if both parents have been working outside the home. Your children need your time and attention.

4. **If possible, stay together to raise your kids.** Two-parent families are the ideal arrangement for raising successful kids. It's more than just a cliché to say that the most important thing a father can do for his children is to love their mother, and the most important thing a mother can do for her children is to love their father.

I believe, if all progressive parents take this four-pronged approach, we will raise positive, successful children!

The Triple 'A' Seal of Good Parenting

Dr. Marlin Howe

Affirmation

A parent's unconditional affirmation involves hundreds of little and big messages each day by the parents which say one thing — that their children are very valuable. On a daily basis parents should try to communicate to their children that they are very worthy. Affirmation communicates to the mind of a child that (s)he is very valuable and important.

Affection

A parent's unconditional affection does for a child's emotion what affirmation does for a child's mind — the child knows that (s)he is greatly loved. Not only does a child ***know*** (s)he is loved, (s)he ***feels*** loved. Children feel emotionally valuable through loving words, hand holding, squeezes, hugs and kisses and looks of endearment. Children usually enjoy receiving affection well into adulthood.

Appreciation

Only when a parent affirms and affects their children may they conditionally appreciate him or her. Affirmation and affection says to the spirit, "I like who you are." Appreciation says to the will, "I like what you do." Praise is one reward that can

never be overdone. Compliment your children. Tell them that they have done a good job, then build up their spirit by telling them how neat they are. Children, however, do not always act praiseworthy. At times, parents will not appreciate what their children do. Discipline is in order. But, discipline should attempt to shape the will without damaging the spirit. Thus, the effective parent must continue to affirm and to give affection even as the child is being disciplined. To do otherwise will embitter the children.

What Makes a Family Strong?

10 traits essential to a strong, happy family

Kay Kuzma

TRAIT 1: COMMITMENT

The most important trait in strong, happy families is commitment. Commitment to the team — putting the family first — and commitment to each individual on the family in helping him or her become everything he or she can. With commitment comes the desire to help family members reach their potential. A winning attitude is, *"I'll forgo my own immediate gratification to help a family member succeed, because I know the personal joy that I experience when I help another family member."*

TRAIT 2: APPRECIATION

Do you let your family members know that they are appreciated? Do you give them positive attention? Strong families focus on the strengths of each other — not the faults. If you think your family needs improvement in this area, try serving a compliment at each practice. *"I really like the way that you...", "One of the things I like best about you is...", "You make me happy when you...", "You have real talent when it comes to...", "You make me proud when you..."*

TRAIT 3: TIME TOGETHER

Healthy families enjoy being together. They work together, play together, and enjoy leisure times

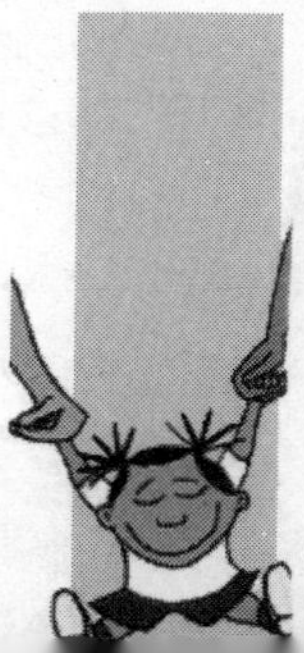

together. They may be very busy, but they plan time together.

TRAIT 4: COMMUNICATION

To understand each other, a family has to be willing to invest the time necessary to share their feelings and opinions. Because you are a product of your experiences, each day you are a new person. Without talking and listening to each other, family members can soon become strangers.

TRAIT 5: RELIGION

Praying together, as well as praying for one another are extremely important for a strong, happy family. Worshipping together is a bonding experience.

TRAIT 6: SENSE OF HUMOUR

Happy families have fun together; they play together; they laugh together. Having a sense of humour during tense, troublesome moments defuses the tension and has an immediate calming effect.

TRAIT 7: SHARE RESPONSIBILITY

Flexibility is an important trait in strong families, especially when it comes to sharing responsibility and roles. If family members do whatever is necessary to meet each other's needs, even if the task does not happen to be on their list, everyone is happier.

T-ogether
E-veryone
A-ccomplishes
M-ore!

TRAIT 8: COMMON INTERESTS

The more that family members have in common, the more they tend to do together. Having similar interests and developing common goals gives the family something to look forward to, to plan toward, and to experience together.

TRAIT 9: SERVICE TO OTHERS

Just as a pond grows stagnant if there is no outlet, so does the family. ***Rosalynn and Jimmy Carter*** agreed that nothing (not even the White House experience) brought them as much joy and satisfaction as they received when pounding nails and painting walls in houses they were volunteering to build for others. Your own problems and worries can become insignificant when seen from the perspective of others who have so much less than you.

TRAIT 10: SEEKING HELP

Healthy families are not problem-free; they just admit to problems and get the help they need to solve them! The longer a problem drags on without a solution, the more discouraging family life becomes. Do not allow this to happen.

When you are a big enough person to admit you are not perfect and when you choose to get the help you need, not only will you gain the respect of your family, but you will find that your goal of living 'happily ever after' is attainable after all.

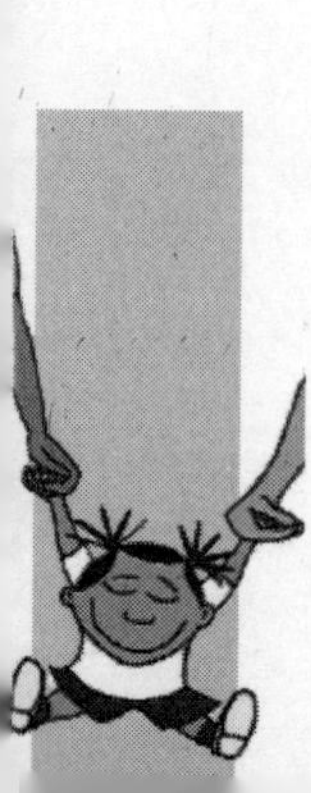

How Can I be a Good Parent?

***Parental Tips from* familydoctor.org**

There's not just one right way to raise children. And there's no such thing as a perfect parent — or a perfect child. But here are some guidelines to help your children grow up healthy and happy:

1. **Show your love.** Every day, tell your children: *"I love you. You're special to me."* Give lots of hugs and kisses.

2. **Listen when your children talk.** Listening to your children tells them that you think they're important and that you're interested in what they have to say.

3. **Make your children feel safe.** Comfort them when they're scared. Show them you've taken steps to protect them.

4. **Provide order in their lives.** Keep a regular schedule of meals, naps and bedtimes. If you have to change the schedule, tell them about the changes ahead of time.

5. **Praise your children.** When your children learn something new or behave well, tell them you're proud of them.

6. **Criticise the behaviour, not the child.** When your child makes a mistake, don't say, *"You were bad."* Instead, explain what the child did wrong. For example, say: *"Running into the street without looking isn't safe."* Then tell the child what to do instead: *"First, look both ways for cars."*

7. **Be consistent.** Your rules don't have to be the same ones other parents have, but they do need to be clear and consistent. (Consistent means the rules are the same all the time.) If two parents are raising a child, both need to use the same rules. Also, make sure baby-sitters and relatives know, and follow, your family rules.

8. **Spend time with your children.** Do things together, like reading, walking, playing and cleaning house. What children want most is your attention. Bad behaviour is usually their way of getting your attention.

Certain Basic Principles on Parenting

Author Unknown (adapted)

1. There should be a **fundamental trust** in the natural goodness of the child. Every parent must know that the child is innocent, born with natural goodness and love, needing protection and caring nurture. Every child's true nature is good, loving, affectionate, and joyfully responsive to gentle and caring treatment.

2. Every home must be **child-centric**, not parent-centred or authority-centred. This means that the home exists primarily to meet the needs of the child. Responsible, mature parents certainly place the needs of the child ahead of their own.

3. The role of the parent is that of **provider and protector** — not controller or teacher or shaper or 'preparer-for-life.' This responsibility includes making the home safe, free from danger, threats and fear — a secure place where children can explore and play, and learn about themselves, their siblings, their parents, and their world.

4. Teaching is done **by example** only, unless specifically requested by the child. The instilling of values, attitudes and character is

done by role-modelling in any case; preaching, do-as-I-say-not-as-I-do admonitions teach only hypocrisy.

5. The child is recognised as **the expert** on what and who a child is, what childhood is like. Others need but to observe and be open to understanding what this child is about and why, instead of trying to force the child into a mould. This requires basic trust in the child's inherent goodness. The child is the teacher, the one from whom we learn.

6. The child comes equipped with a drive for **self-directed learning** — with a fierce eagerness to understand the world and everything in it — but on their own terms and at their own pace. Therefore ***'child's play'*** is the child's serious work, to be respected by all parents. The essential need is to provide a safe place for doing that exploring, discovering, and experiencing, free from fear of reprimand, rejection, and threat of punishment or risk of hurt. Parents follow the child's lead in the quest for self-teaching, and avoid directing or controlling, but rather stand by to assist and facilitate when asked to do so, and to acknowledge the new knowledge.

7. The harm done by all forms of **punishment** is recognised, and prohibited absolutely. Punishment of any form — corporal or psychological — does more harm than good.

The benefits of non-punitive parenting are so immediately evident, and the surprising boost in self-respect is so helpful, that parents ask themselves how they ever indulged in the punishment mindset to begin with.

8. The child's **self-esteem is protected** as carefully as their physical wellbeing. Respect for this developing individual, his or her unique self-identity, is paramount. There is no down-putting, no 'bad girl' and 'bad boy,' nor is there praise, as in 'good girl' or 'good boy' judgements. Praise and put-downs are equally harmful to self-esteem. Anyone who can praise can, in the next breath, condemn.

9. The **child is a mirror**, reflecting the viewer's attractive qualities as well the negative. That which we hate in ourselves, unconsciously, we tend to see in the child. The liar is furious when his/her child tells a lie; the shoplifter is outraged when the child takes what is not his. To be mindful of that is to forgo punishing, seeing the unfairness of making the child suffer for one's own character defects. The up side is feeling the joy of seeing love and affection reflected in the child.

10. The hierarchical structure of the family must be **democratic**. Practically, in all Indian families, the family is organised with all authority in the parents; leaving the children

to fight for rights, respect, and a measure of self-direction. If the child is to grow in responsibility and discipline, he or she must enjoy the rights of full membership in the family organisation.

Since democracy is the governing body in a family, there is no commanding, no issuing of orders, no meting out of rewards and punishments by the boss or the head.

In Democratic Discipline, grievances are heard at family meetings, rights protected disputes resolved, and recommendations and suggestions made, usually by consensus. It will indeed be a joy for children to live in such families.

Parental Love: A Boon for Life

Vijai P. Sharma

Everybody knows that in order to survive and thrive, babies need loving and caring parents, but few know that feeling loved and being close to parents in early years helps us in sickness and health in later life — positive health effects can be seen at 30, 40 or even later.

In the early 1950s, 126 healthy **Harvard University** students were randomly asked to describe how they felt about their parents. They were to rate their relationship with mother and father as, 'very close,' 'warm and friendly,' 'tolerant,' or 'strained and cold.'

After 35 years, medical records were obtained on these participants. An amazing 91% who, 35 years earlier, felt that their relationship with their mothers was just tolerable, or strained and cold. had developed serious diseases in mid-life, including coronary artery disease, high blood pressure, ulcers, and alcoholism. By comparison, only 45% of those who had earlier reported warm and friendly relationship with parents had similar illnesses.

Furthermore, all the participants (literally, 100%) who had described their relationship with both parents as 'less than warm' had serious diseases

diagnosed in midlife as compared to only 47% of those who had felt their parents were 'warm and close.'

Researchers concluded that parental love seems to act as a buffer against later life illnesses. They speculated that the foundation of loving parental relationship helps to lessen the negative impact of stress and pathogens in later life, protect the immune system, and strengthen the desire to live and heal.

In a related study, male medical students studying at **Johns Hopkins University** were evaluated for closeness to their parents. Over a period of several years, researchers collected this information on 1,100 students. Follow up of their health records covered a span of thirty, forty, or in some cases, fifty years. Results were similar to those of the Harvard study. Medical students, who subsequently developed cancer, were more likely to have described a lack of closeness with their parents thirty, forty, or fifty years earlier.

The researchers in the above study found that no other factor was more significantly related to illness than the degree of parental closeness reported in the earlier years. Even smoking, drinking, or exposure to harmful substances were less significant than parental closeness in predicting who is likely to develop serious illness later.

Our understanding of physical illnesses has been expanding. Just a few years ago, we viewed illnesses such as cancer, heart disease, or diabetes, as consequences of our current unhealthy behaviours. They were referred to as the 'lifestyle diseases.' The term 'lifestyle,' basically, refers to the behaviours and choices we make during our adult lives. Lately, our understanding of diseases has taken us a little further and deeper, tracing the origin of some illnesses right down to childhood.

For example, we now know that children who habitually smoke, drink, and abuse drugs, or who are overweight 'couch potatoes,' are more likely to develop medical complications in later life. Medical researchers have followed children in their adult years and have observed this to be true. But this is only half the story. What about the emotional experiences of children? Do they have an impact on health? The Harvard and Johns Hopkins' studies suggest they do.

We are physical, mental and spiritual beings. Health and happiness result from our pursuit of physical, mental, and spiritual development. The so-called lifestyle diseases result from an imbalance of, or lack of development in any or all three aspects. A child who is emotionally deprived is not given all the tools needed to work for a happy and healthy adulthood.

Does this mean that if our parents were warm and loving during our childhood, we don't need to bother to eat right or live right? No, we still will have to work to maintain good health. Does it mean that if our parents were cold or uncaring, there is no point of trying to live healthily because we are going to develop some horrible illness anyway? No, because how we relate to others, help others and love them today have definite positive effects on our health tomorrow.

As our understanding of illnesses expands, it places a greater responsibility on us for our health. For example, parents should know that if they emotionally hold themselves back from their children, the latter may pay a physical, emotional, and spiritual price for the rest of their lives.

It has been said that all parents should give their children two things: roots and wings.

How can I Discipline my Young Child?

First Years Last Forever

Canadian Institute of Child Health

Don't expect young children to do what you say all the time. Young children are normally impulsive and will hit, yell, or fall apart at times because their feelings of frustration and anger exceed their ability to control themselves. Helping them learn self-control is a long-term process. It is also normal for children to 'test' a rule by breaking it. When you respond in a supportive, consistent way, you are helping your child to feel safe in the world.

Many approaches to setting limits can work, as long as they are intended to help and teach children, rather than to punish them. Keep these ideas in mind:

- Communicate to your child what needs to be done at that moment: *"I know you're having fun at the park, but it's time to get ready to go now."*

- Redirect your child's attention or activity by using neutral or positive language: *"It's not okay to draw on the wall, but here is some paper you can use."*

- Say no while maintaining love: *"I love you, but I don't love what you're doing."*

- Give the reason for your rule: *"Don't run with scissors — you might fall and hurt yourself!"*

- Give limited tasks and be specific: *"Please pick up your stuffed animals..."* (instead of *'Please clean up your room.'*)

- Acknowledge children's feelings, but set limits: *"I know you're angry, but no biting..."*

- Help children see how their actions affect others: *"Your sister is upset because you pinched her. How would you feel if she hurt you?"*

- Help children see how they can use their words to communicate their feelings: *"Tell your brother you don't like it when he hits you."*

- Acknowledge positive behaviour: *"You did a good job picking up your stuffed animals. Thank you."*

7 Steps to Being A Good Parent

Teresa, (The CuteKid™)

What makes a good parent? Good parents don't just happen. Good parents grow and apply lessons that they have learned. They are continually trying to improve themselves and their parenting skills.

Author and Paediatrician **Marianne Neifert** shares the seven things that will help you understand what makes a good parent.

1. ***Provide unconditional love and encouragement to your child.*** Saying *"I love you"* is important. But even more important is showing your child that you love them by giving your time and attention. Playing games, reading stories, and talking all show your love. Encouragement is also essential. Every child needs to feel like their parents are their best cheerleader and can accomplish anything.

2. ***Make your kids a high priority.*** This doesn't mean that you don't take care of yourself and your marriage. But it does mean that your children should come before others. This may mean that you need to say 'No' sometimes. I have a hard time saying 'No' and I often have to remind myself that if I say 'Yes' I will be placing my children lower on my priority list.

3. ***Strengthen your team.*** Strengthening your team applies to parents. It means that parents agree beforehand on **important issues like rules and discipline.** They discuss together important decisions that need to be made concerning the children and family.

4. ***Discipline consistently.*** To cultivate this quality of being a good parent is one of the hardest things to do. At the end of a hard day it is so easy to give in to a child that is crying or whining, but that is not consistent. It does not teach them and only makes your job as a parent more difficult. **Set limits and rules and always enforce them.**

5. ***Teach responsibility.*** Give your children responsibilities. My son is required to make his own bed. He also empties the small garbage cans every week. All my children are responsible for helping clean up the house and clearing their dishes off of the table. Children need to understand that they are responsible for their own actions and the consequences that follow. I often tell my children, *"No one can make you mad, you choose how you react."*

6. ***Create togetherness through routines.*** Daily, weekly, or even yearly family rituals create a bond between family members. It may be as simple as reading a book together every night

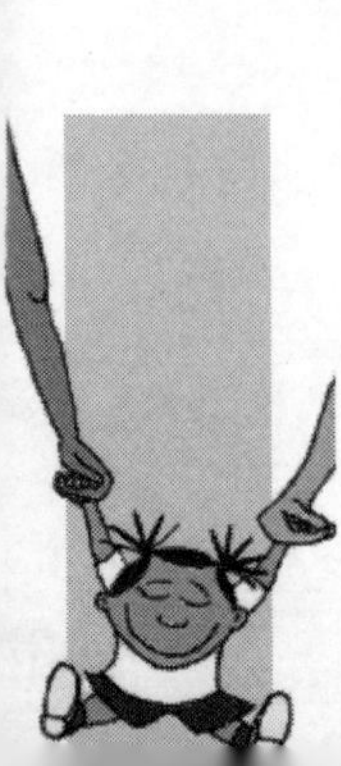

or taking a yearly trip to the beach. Our family eats pizza and watches a movie every Friday night. Dr. Neifert says rituals provide the *"social glue that bonds one generation to another, creating many of the special anchor memories within a family."*

7. ***Take time to recharge.*** Parents need to take some time for themselves. When you are running on empty you are not doing your children any good. *"Sleep deprivation, isolation and self-neglect can leave parents feeling physically depleted, emotionally discouraged and ineffective."* My husband and I spend time together every evening after putting our children in bed. We also have a date night every Saturday night, though it usually consists of watching a movie or playing games at home, we take the time to be together.

Now that you know the seven steps to being a good parent the hard part begins, actually applying it. So take it one step at a time.

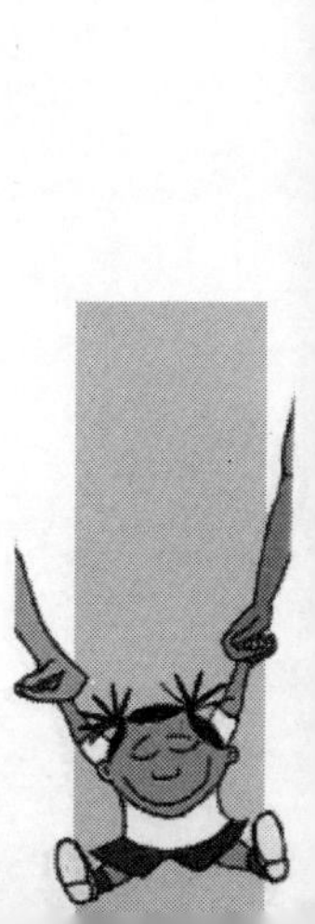

10 Things Parents should Know about Teenagers

Author Unknown

1. **It's not easy being a teenager**
   Teenagers want independence and to be treated like adults, but often lack the necessary maturity, which only comes through experience. They need some independence, coupled with guidance. Give them freedom of choice in matters that will help them mature, yet won't seriously harm them or others when they make wrong choices.

2. **Teens are in a process of continual change**
   Just as teens need lots of good food, lots of sleep, and lots of exercise to meet the needs of their growing bodies, they need lots of positive input to grow emotionally and intellectually.

3. **Each teen is different and has individual needs**
   Most teenagers go through the same phases, but at different ages and with varying degrees of difficulty. Treat them as individuals.

4. **Upbeat is better**
   If you only talk to your teens when you need to reprimand them, they will avoid you. Establish positive communication when they are younger and keep it up as they get older,

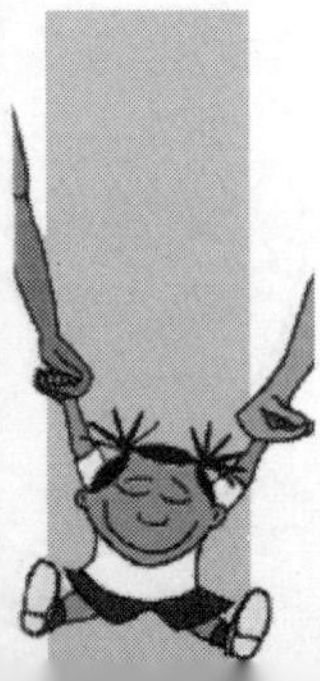

and they will be more likely to receive direction from you during the tough teen years.

5. **Balance between fun and responsibility**
   Help your teens grow into adulthood by teaching them to put responsibility before having fun, and reward them with fun activities when they do.

6. **Teens need clearly-defined limits**
   Teens often test the limits set for them to see how much they can get away with. Discuss the rules together, agree if you can, and then enforce them lovingly but firmly.

7. **Teens need space**
   In their attempt to establish their own identity, it is normal for teenagers to distance themselves from their parents. Don't take it personally. Let them flap their wings, within reasonable limits, but make sure they know you're always there for them.

8. **Teens need to feel fulfilled**
   Help your teens set goals for themselves that are worthwhile, challenging, and attainable, and then help them achieve their goals.

9. **Peer pressure is strongest in teen years**
   Your teens' friends can influence, so get to know them and try to bring out the best in them.

10. **Teens need to feel understood**

    You may not understand them any better than they understand themselves, but God does. Hearing them out and then taking their problems to God together will go a lot further than you trying to supply them with all the answers yourself.

PART III

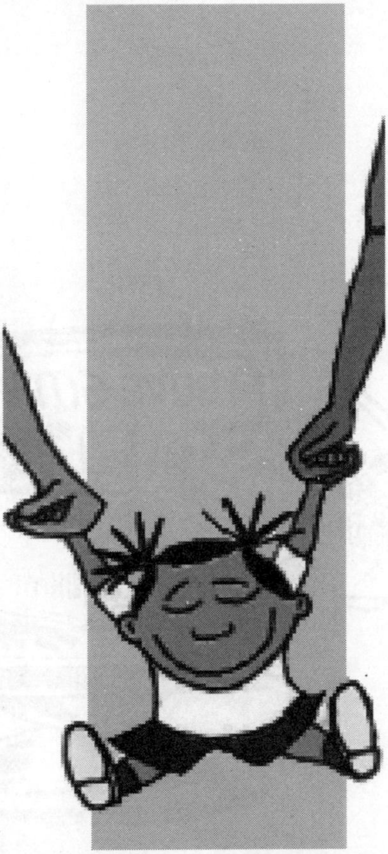

MAILWISE

YOU'VE GOT MAIL

10 Keys to Being a Happy Parent

1. Be the first to say "Hello!"

2. Live beneath your means.

3. Treat your children as you would want to be treated.

4. Never give up on any child; miracles are known to happen all the time.

5. Be tough-minded, kind and tender hearted.

6. Don't forget that a child's greatest emotional need is to feel appreciated.

7. Keep your promises.

8. Learn to demonstrate cheerfulness even when you don't feel it.

9. Don't miss an opportunity to tell your children you love them.

10. Compliment your children every day.

A Challenge for the 21st Century Parent

Adapted from Lou Torok

It's a challenge for 21st century parents...

- ⌘ To replace darkness with light,
- ⌘ To replace hatred with love,
- ⌘ To replace suspicion with trust,
- ⌘ To replace lies and hypocrisy with honesty,
- ⌘ To replace abuse with kindness,
- ⌘ To replace frustration with patience,
- ⌘ To replace fear with understanding,
- ⌘ To replace bias, prejudice and discrimination with tolerance,
- ⌘ To replace ignorance with knowledge,
- ⌘ To replace indifference with concern,
- ⌘ And to replace apathy with action.

A Child's Advice to His Parents

Source Unknown

My hands are small. Please don't expect perfection whenever I make a bed, draw a picture, or throw a ball.

My eyes have not seen the world as yours have. Please let me explore it at my own level without unnecessary restrictions.

Housework will always be there, but I will be little only for a short time. Please take time to explain about this wonderful world.

My feelings are tender. Please be sensitive to my needs. Treat me as you would like to be treated.

I am a special gift from God. Treasure me as God intended, holding me accountable for my actions, giving me guidelines to live by, and disciplining me in a loving manner.

I need your encouragement to grow, so go easy on the criticism. Try to correct my behaviour without criticising me as a person.

Give me the freedom to make decisions. Permit me to fail, so I can learn from my mistakes. Then I'll be prepared to make the kind of decisions life requires of me as an adult.

Don't redo jobs that I have already done. This makes me feel that my efforts don't quite measure up to your expectations. I know it's hard, but please don't compare me with my brother or sister.

Please don't be afraid to leave for a weekend together. Kids need vacations from parents, just as parents need to get away occasionally. This is also a great way to show us kids that your marriage is very special.

Please set a good example by taking me to a worship centre regularly. I enjoy learning more about God.

A Father's Advice to His Son

Author Unknown

When Eric was getting ready to return to school after the summer break, his Dad gave him some sheets of paper containing hand-written words of advice for further reflection. A number of Eric's friends asked if they, too, could read these words of wisdom from a father to his son.

1. Dwell on the future, not the past. What's done is done, the future is the only thing you can have an impact on.

2. Ask God for forgiveness and move on. God always forgives the faithful.

3. Don't feel as though you must bare your soul to others. This puts a burden on them. Go on a 'need to know' basis.

4. This too will pass, if you want it to. Mature, healthy relationships combat the desire to falter.

5. Take solace from your relationship with God and those you love.

6. Focus on the positive and use it. Reflect on your gains and build on your strengths. Let go of your failures.

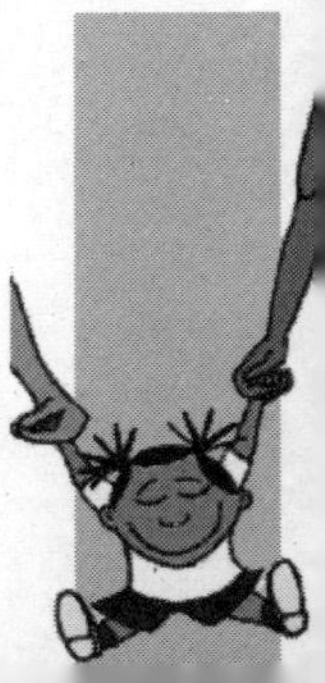

7. Nobody is perfect, not even you (or me). There will always be failings and temptations. That's what the Devil does for a living!

8. Count your blessings, nurture your faith. Thank God everyday for who you are. Move on through this earthly existence as best you can.

9. Enjoy life! Leave a legacy for your children to follow. That's all we really can do.

10. I love you.

Son, Forgive Me!

Adapted from W. Livingston Larned

Son, I am saying this as you lie asleep, one little hand crumpled under your cheek. Just a few minutes ago, as I sat reading my paper, a wave of remorse swept over me and drove me to your bedside.

These are the things I was thinking, son: I had spoken crossly to you. I scolded you as you were getting ready for school because you gave your face merely a dab with a towel. I took you to task for not cleaning your shoes. I called out angrily when you threw some of your things on the floor.

At breakfast I found fault, too. You spilled things. You gulped down your food. You put your elbows on the table.

As you started off to play and I left for work, you turned and waved a hand and called, "Goodbye, Daddy!"
"Stand up straight!" was my goodbye.

Then it began all over again in the late afternoon. As I came up the road, I spied you down on your knees, playing marbles. There were holes in the knees of your pants. I humiliated you in front of your friends by making you come in the house. Pants are expensive, and if you had to pay for

them yourself you wouldn't wear them out by crawling around on the ground. Imagine that, son, from a father!

Do you remember later, when I was reading and you came in timidly, with a hurt look in your eyes? When I glanced up over my paper, impatient at the interruption, you hesitated at the door. "What is it you want?" I snapped. You said nothing, but ran across the room and in one tempestuous plunge, threw your arms around my neck and kissed me. Your small arms tightened with an affection that God had set blooming in your heart and which even my neglect could not wither. And then you were gone, pattering up the stairs.

Well, son, it was shortly afterwards that my paper slipped from my hands and a terrible sickening feeling came over me. I realised I'd fallen into a horrible habit — the habit of finding fault, of reprimanding. This was my reward to you for being a boy. It wasn't that I didn't love you; it was that I expected too much of you at your age. I was measuring you by the yardstick of my own years.

Meanwhile, your love for me was as big and bright and unstoppable as the dawn. Your spontaneous goodnight kiss showed me that. And so I have come to your bedside and I knelt here in the darkness, ashamed. It's a feeble atonement.

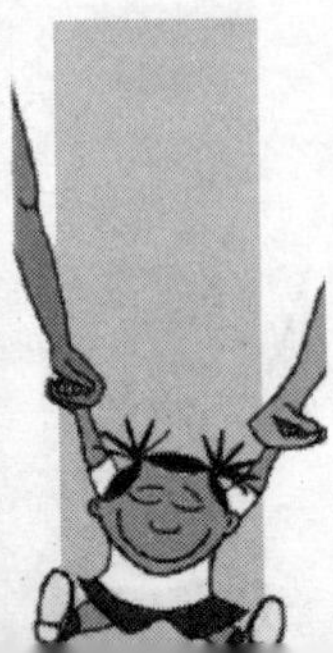

Tomorrow I will be a real daddy! I will play with you and share your ups and downs. I will bite my tongue when impatient words come. I will remember that you are a little boy, and won't ask too much.

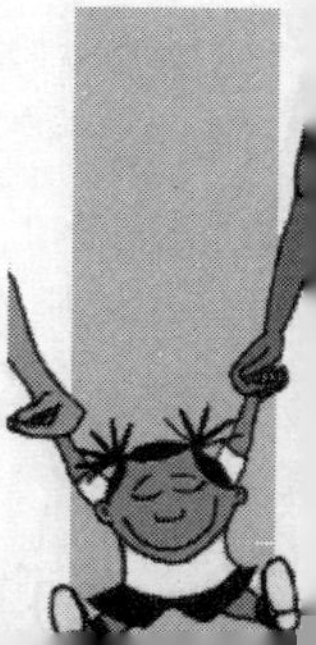

12 Golden Rules for Living

Source Unknown

1. If you open it,
   close it.
2. If you turn it on,
   turn it off.
3. If you unlock it,
   lock it up.
4. If you break it,
   admit it.
5. If you can't fix it,
   call in someone who can.
6. If you borrow it,
   return it.
7. If you value it,
   take care of it.
8. If you make a mess,
   clean it up.
9. If you move it,
   put it back.
10. If it belongs to someone else,
    get permission to use it.
11. If you don't know how to operate it,
    leave it alone.
12. If it's none of your business,
    don't ask questions.

Love in the Home

Author Unknown

If I live in a house of spotless beauty with everything in its place, but have not Love, I am a housekeeper — not a homemaker.

If I have time for waxing, polishing, and decorative achievements, but have not Love, my children learn cleanliness — not godliness.

Love leaves the dust in search of a child's laugh.

Love smiles at the tiny fingerprints on a newly cleaned window.

Love wipes away the tears before it wipes up the spilled milk.

Love picks up the child before it picks up the toys.

Love is present through the trials.

Love reprimands, reproves, and is responsive.

Love crawls with the baby, walks with the toddler, runs with the child, then stands aside to let the youth walk into adulthood.

Love is the key that opens salvation's message to a child's heart.

Before I became a mother, I took glory in my house of perfection. Now I glory in God's perfection of my child. As a mother, there is much I must teach my child, but the greatest of all is Love.

Mum's Love

Source Unknown

When you were one, she fed you and bathed you. You thanked her by crying all night long.

When you were two, she taught you to walk. You thanked her by running away when she called.

When you were three, she made all your meals with love. You thanked her by tossing your plate on the floor.

When you were four, she gave you some crayons. You thanked her by colouring the dining room table.

When you were five, she dressed you for the holidays. You thanked her by plopping into the nearest puddle.

When you were six, she walked you to school. You thanked her by screaming, ***"I'm not going!"***

When you were seven, she bought you a baseball. You thanked her by throwing it through the next-door neighbour's window.

When you were eight, she handed you an ice cream. You thanked her by dripping it all over your lap.

When you were nine, she paid for piano lessons. You thanked her by never even bothering to practise.

When you were 10, she drove you all day, from soccer to gymnastics to one birthday party after another; you thanked her by jumping out of the car and never looking back.

When you were 11, she took you and your friends to the movies; you thanked her by asking her to sit in a different row.

When you were 12, she warned you not to watch certain TV shows. You thanked her by waiting until she left the house.

When you were 13, she suggested a haircut. You thanked her by telling her she had no taste.

When you were 14, she paid for a month away at summer camp. You thanked her by forgetting to write a single letter.

When you were 15, she came home from work, looking for a hug. You thanked her by having your bedroom door locked.

When you were 16, she taught you how to drive her car. You thanked her by taking it every chance you could.

When you were 17, she was expecting an important call. You thanked her by talking on the phone all night.

When you were 18, she cried at your high school graduation. You thanked her by staying out partying until dawn.

When you were 19, she paid for your college tuition, drove you to campus, carried your bags. You thanked her by saying good-bye outside the dorm so you wouldn't be embarrassed in front of your friends.

When you were 20, she asked whether you were seeing anyone. You thanked her by saying, ***"It's none of your business."***

When you were 21, she suggested certain careers for your future. You thanked her by saying, ***"I don't want to be like you."***

When you were 22, she hugged you at your college graduation. You thanked her by asking whether she could pay for a trip to Europe.

When you were 23, she gave you furniture for your first apartment. You thanked her by telling your friends it was old-fashioned.

When you were 24, she met your fiancé and asked about your plans for the future. You thanked her by glaring and growling, ***"Muuhh-ther, please!"*** When you were 25, she helped to pay for your wedding, and she cried and told you how deeply she loved you. You thanked her by moving halfway across the country.

When you were 30, she called with some advice on the baby. You thanked her by telling her, ***"Things are different now."***

When you were 40, she called to remind you of relative's birthday. You thanked her by saying you were ***"really busy right now."***

When you were 50, she fell ill and needed you to take care of her. You thanked her by reading about the burden parents become to their children.

And then, one day, she quietly died. And everything you never did came crashing down like thunder on your heart!

If she's still around, love her more than ever; if she's not, remember her unconditional love and pass it on. Love your Mother in her lifetime, she's the only one you'll ever have!

Reflections of a Father

Charles (Pop) Avery

I can...

... give you life, but I can't live it for you.

... teach you things, but can't make you learn.

... give you directions, but can't be there to lead.

... allow you freedom, but can't account for it.

... take you to church, but can't make you believe.

... teach you right from wrong, but can't always decide for you.

... buy you beautiful clothes, but can't make you beautiful inside.

... offer you advice, but can't accept it for you.

... offer you love, but can't force it upon you.

... teach you to share, but can't make you unselfish.

... teach you respect, but can't force you to show honour.

... advise you about friends, but can't choose them for you.

... advise you about sex, but can't keep you pure.

... teach you the facts of life, but can't build your reputation.

... tell you about drink, but can't say *'no'* for you.

... warn you about drugs, but can't prevent you from using them.

... tell you about lofty goals, but can't achieve them for you.

... teach you about kindness, but can't force you to be gracious.

... warn you about sins, but can't make you moral.

... love you as a child, but can't place you in God's family.

... pray for you, but I cannot make you walk with God.

... teach you about God, but can't make Him your Lord.

... tell you how to live, but can't give you eternal life.

... love you unconditionally all of my life

...and will!

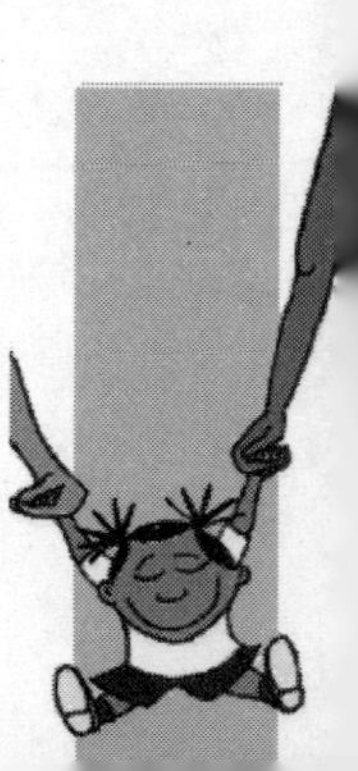

The Paradox of our Age

Adapted from Bob Moorehead

We...

... have taller buildings, but shorter tempers;

... have wider freeways, but narrower viewpoints;

... spend more, but have less;

... buy more, but enjoy it less.

... have bigger houses but smaller families;

... have more conveniences, but less time;

... have more degrees, but less sense;

... have more knowledge, but less judgment;

... have more experts, but less solutions;

... have more medicine, but less health.

... have multiplied our possessions, but reduced our values.

... talk too much, love too seldom and hate too often.

... have learned how to make a living, but not a life;

... have added years to life, not life to years.

... have been all the way to the moon and back,

but have trouble crossing the street to meet our neighbour.

... have conquered outer space, but not inner space;

... have done larger things, but not better things;

... have split the atom, but not our prejudice.

... have higher incomes, but lower morale;

... are long on quantity, but short on quality.

... live in the times of tall men, and short character; steep profits, and shallow relationships.

... have arrived in a time of world peace, but domestic violence;

... have more leisure, but less fun;

... have more kinds of food, but less nutrition.

... join our earnings through two incomes, but end up divorced;

... live in fancier houses, but broken homes.

... are in an era when there is so much in the showroom window, but nothing in stock!

Rules from God for Parents and Children

Source Unknown

1. Wake Up! Decide to make it a good day.
   "This is the day the Lord has made; let us be glad and rejoice in it."

   Psalms 118:24

2. Dress Up! The best way to dress up is to put on a smile. A smile is an inexpensive way to improve your looks.
   "Not as man sees does God see, because man sees the appearance but the Lord looks in to the heart."

   I Samuel 16:7

3. Listen Up! Say nice things and learn to listen. God gave us two ears and one mouth, so He must have meant for us to do twice as much listening as talking.
   "He who guards his mouth protects his life..."

   Proverbs 13:3

4. Stand Up! For what you believe in. Stand for something or you will fall for anything.
   "Let us not grow tired of doing good, for in due time we shall reap our harvest, if we do not give up. So then, while we have the opportunity, let us do good to all..."

   Galatians 6:9-10

5. Look Up! To the Lord.
   "I have the strength for everything through Him who empowers me."

   Philippians 4:13

6. Reach Up! For something higher.
   "Trust in the Lord with all your heart, and on your own intelligence rely not. In all your ways be mindful of Him, and He will make straight your paths."

   Proverbs 3:5-6

7. Lift Up! Your Prayers.
   "Have no anxiety at all, but in everything, by prayer and petition...make your requests known to God."

   Philippians 4:6

When you Thought I wasn't Looking

Mary Rita Schilke Korzan

When you thought I wasn't looking,
I saw you hang my first painting on the refrigerator, and even though I knew it wasn't all that great I really wanted to paint another one.

When you thought I wasn't looking,
I saw you feed a stray cat, and I thought it was good to be kind to animals.

When you thought I wasn't looking,
I saw you make my favourite cake just for me, and I knew that little things are special.

When you thought I wasn't looking,
I heard you say a prayer, and I believed there is a God I could always talk to.

When you thought I wasn't looking,
I felt you kiss me goodnight, and I felt loved for what I was rather than what I had.

When you thought I wasn't looking,
I saw tears well up in your eyes, and learned that sometimes things hurt, but it's okay to cry.

When you thought I wasn't looking,
I saw that you cared, and wanted to be everything that I could be.

When you thought I wasn't looking
I looked — and wanted to say thanks for all the things I saw when you thought I wasn't looking.

The Steps of a Child

Dorothy Law Nolte

If a child lives with...

... criticism, he learns to condemn.

... hostility, he learns to fight.

... ridicule, he learns to be shy.

... shame, he learns to feel guilty.

... tolerance, he learns to be patient.

... encouragement, he learns confidence.

... praise, he learns to appreciate.

... fairness, he learns justice.

... approval, he learns to like himself.

... acceptance and friendship, he learns to find love in the world.

If I had my Child to Raise all over Again

Diane Loomans

If I had my child to raise all over again,

I'd build self-esteem first,
and the house later.

I'd finger-paint more,
and point the finger less.

I'd do less correcting
and more connecting.

I'd take my eyes off my watch,
and watch with my eyes.

I'd take more hikes
and fly more kites.

I'd stop playing serious,
and seriously play.

I'd run through more fields
and gaze at more stars.

I'd do more hugging
and less tugging.

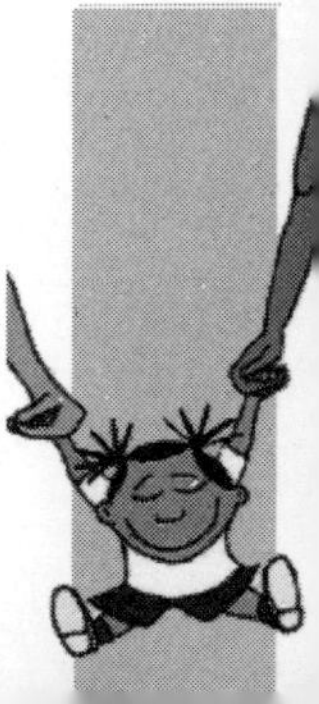

The Images of a Mother

Anonymous

4 years : My Mommy can do anything!

8 years : My Mom knows a lot! A whole lot!

12 years : My Mother doesn't really know quite everything.

14 years : Naturally, Mother doesn't know that, either.

16 years : Mother? She's hopelessly old-fashioned.

18 years : That old woman? She's way out of date!

25 years : Well, she might know a little bit about it.

35 years : Before we decide, let's get Mom's opinion.

45 years : Wonder what Mom would have thought about it?

65 years : If Mom was still alive; I could have talked it over with her!

A Parent's Prayer

Abigail Van Buren

Heavenly Father,
Make me a better parent
Teach me to understand my children,
To listen patiently to what they have to say,
And to answer all their questions kindly.
Keep me from interrupting them,
or contradicting them.
Make me as courteous to them
as I would have them be to me.
Forbid that I should ever laugh at their mistakes,
Or resort to shame or ridicule
if they displease me.
Bless me with the bigness to grant them
all their reasonable requests,
And the courage to deny them privileges
that I know will do them harm.
Make me fair and just and kind.
And fit me, O Lord,
to be loved and respected
and imitated by my children.
Amen

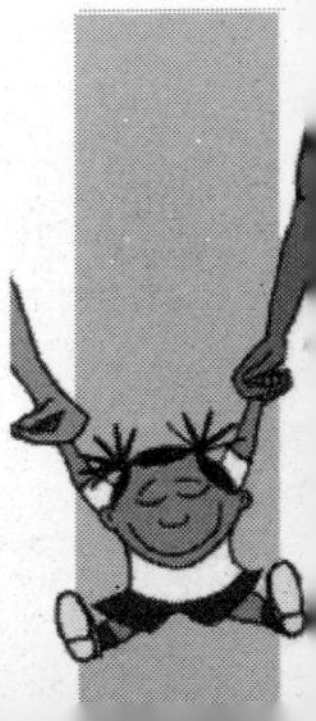

Suggested Resources

10 Best Gifts for your Teen | ***Patt and Steve Saso***
9 Myths that Damage a Child's Confidence | ***Pat Holt***
Confident Children: Help them feel good about themselves | ***Gael Lindenfield***
Keys to Parenting (A 5-book series) | ***Derek & Michelle Brooks***
Parenting Teenagers for Positive Results | ***Jim Burns***
Parents' Guide to the Spiritual Mentoring of Teens | ***Joe White and Jim Weidmann***
Recipes for Parenting | ***Pervin Dadachanji***
Smart Parenting | ***Peter Favaro***
Taking Care of Me | ***Mary Kay Mueller***
What do you really want for your Children | ***Wayne W. Dyer***
When Kids are Mad, not Bad | ***Henry A Paul***
Bringing up a Dream Child | ***Juhi Agarwal***

Other Books by the Author

He Can Who Thinks He Can
The Way to Success and Happiness
An Elocution Manual
On the Way Home
Catholic Catechism for School Children

Author's Address
Don Bosco Youth Centre
Laitumkhrah
Shillong - 793 003,
Meghalaya, India
jparankimalil@gmail.com | johny@sancharnet.in